Praise for

The Good Steward

I have been asked more times than I can count how to increase generosity in the church. The reality is that generosity is a function of one thing and that is faithful Stewards functioning as faithful stewards with the financial resources entrusted to them by our Lord and Savior. As Tim points out however, stewardship really begins with the recognition of God's ownership of all resources, you can't be a steward over something that you own. I've often taught and preached a message that Tim repeats very well and that is that we need to help Christians in the transformation of their heart and minds to one of stewardship of everything. I recommend this book as not only challenging spiritually but also extraordinarily practical. It communicates well how to practice faithful stewardship with financial resources. It is the only way that anyone can experience financial freedom.

—**Ron Blue,** Founder or Co-founder of *Blue & Co, National Chrisitan Foundation, and Kingdom Advisors*

***

Roy and Tim's commitment to teaching Biblical Stewardship is well-documented. This very readable book provides a mix of biblically based concepts, practical applications, and stories from their life for those who've not gotten to their seminar or just want a refresher. I particularly appreciate their expansion of the concept of stewardship to include time, expertise and networks. And the chapter on the power, and importance, of teaching these principles to children and grandchildren feels particularly timely.

—**Jon D. Eisenberg**, President, *National Chrisitan Foundation Lancaster Office*

***

In 'The Good Steward,' Tim and Roy Russell provide **a deeply biblical and refreshingly practical guide to managing wealth with wisdom and faith.** Their framework of the Five Biblical Financial Priorities offers a clear, scriptural approach to financial decision-making—one that leads not only to greater financial stability but also to a deeper trust in God rather than our wealth. This book powerfully affirms that wise stewardship and generous giving are not in conflict but are, in fact, essential partners in the life of a faithful believer. My prayer is that those who apply these timeless principles will one day hear the words, 'Well done, my good and faithful servant.' I highly recommend this book to anyone seeking to align their financial life with God's eternal purposes.

—**Rob West**, CEO, *Kingdom Advisors* and Host of the nationally syndicated radio show *Faith & Finance with Rob West*

***

Roy and Tim Russell have written one of the most comprehensive books that exist on money, wealth, investing, and just plain living. With many Old and New Testament references, this book is a practical guide to getting organized and living a generous life as a "Good Steward". Following the principles outlined and illustrated raises the probability of hearing those sought-after words, "Well done, good and faithful servant." Thank you, Russells, for this primer on so many important financial subjects!

—**Bob Doll**, CEO/CIO of *Crossmark Global Investments*

***

This book is full of practical advice, biblical references, and easy-to-follow instructions on the proper uses of money. It is a wonderful blend of theology and money management!

This book will help you to unbundle your net worth from your self-worth and put money in its proper biblical perspective so that one day you might hear those precious words from our Lord, 'Well done good and faithful servant.

—**Jeffrey Cave**, CIMA®, CKA® Eventide Asset Management

***

I've long had enormous respect for Tim Russell and his father, Roy. Now, reading their book, this has only increased. What biblical wisdom; what practical savvy! Their pages on financing retirement have launched my wife and me into helpful discussion. Their creativity on training children to handle money made us wish we had stumbled on such a gem years ago. I really can't recommend it highly enough.

—**Steve Estes**, Pastor and author

***

What the Russells accomplish in this labor is a tour de force for household sanity, and they achieve this by offering a thorough biblical worldview of stewardship.

—**Uriesou (Uri) Brito**, Pastor and Author

***

There may be people who are better theologians than Tim, and there may be people more skilled in the area of finance and investing than Tim, but in my opinion, Tim Russell's combination of theology and finance is unparalleled. I'm certain that this work will serve the church and the kingdom of God well for years to come.

—**Chuck Vuolo**, Pastor

***

I wholeheartedly and enthusiastically endorse "The Good Steward" by Tim and Roy Russell. My years of working alongside them have given me firsthand insight into the transformative power of the biblical stewardship principles they share. I have the distinct privilege of teaching these principles with Tim on the Stewardology Podcast and through Life Institute's nationwide 'Stewardship Lifestyle Seminar,' where we've seen countless lives and financial situations experience genuine renewal. This book masterfully distills that wisdom into a practical, accessible, and biblically sound guide. If you're ready to align your finances with your faith and unlock more than just financial freedom, I cannot recommend "The Good Steward" highly enough.

—**Rev. Drew Gysi**, Ministry Director at *Life Institute* & Co-host of the *Stewardology Podcast*

The Good Steward

Biblical Principles of Wealth Management

by

Tim Russell and Roy Russell

Published by KHARIS PUBLISHING, an imprint of
KHARIS MEDIA LLC.

Copyright © 2025 Tim Russell and Roy Russell

ISBN-13: 978-1-63746-378-9
ISBN-10: 1-63746-325-1

Library of Congress Control Number: 2025934274

All KHARIS PUBLISHING products are available at special quantity
discounts for bulk purchase for sales promotions, premiums, fund-raising,
and educational needs. For details, contact:
Kharis Media LLC
Tel: 1-630-909-3405
support@kharispublishing.com
www.kharispublishing.com

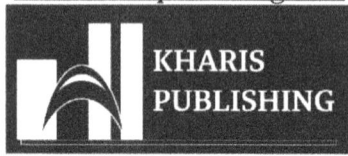

Disclosure & Legal Disclaimer

Table of Contents

Introduction

You've wondered what it means to be a good steward. You believe you have a working budget, but wonder how you could be doing even better. You've experienced the discouragement of working hard, but having little money and savings to show for it. You've run out of money before you reached the end of the month. You've longed to be able to donate money to the church, missions, or charitable organizations, but struggled to scrounge up enough money for a donation. You are not alone!

▯▯▯

Susan is one of our long-time clients. She's like many people we meet in our profession. She is committed to living out her faith, and wants all of her choices to bring glory to God. Before we started working with her, however, when it came to her money she didn't see a clear connection between how she handled it and her Christian convictions. Sure, she gave to her church, but beyond that, as long as she wasn't using her money to fuel a wicked lifestyle, she thought she could spend it however she pleased.

As a result, Susan was never able to get ahead. She always seemed to run out of money before the end of the month. She worked hard, but had little to show for it and had almost no savings. She thought there had to be a better way.

We have witnessed a significant transformation in Susan's life as we've worked with her over the years. The change started as she began to see how her spending decisions impacted many areas of her life. We commended her for giving to her church, but we also shared that the Bible —God's Word—had practical things to say about how we should handle our money. She learned to prioritize her spending through the *Five Biblical Financial Priorities* that you'll learn in Chapter 3. This fresh perspective helped her stop living paycheck to paycheck, build her reserves, and have money to spend on some of the nicer things in life.

Before understanding these basic principles, Susan never thought she'd be able to retire. But now, she is comfortably retired and serving her church, family, and community in ways she never thought possible. She doesn't have all the money she'd like to have, but all of her needs are met, and she is at peace knowing that since the Lord is her Shepherd, she shall not want.

The Church's View of Money

The famous line from Spider-Man, "with great power comes great responsibility," could well apply to the church today. Many of us are living in relative wealth and luxury compared to those living just a hundred years ago. Here in America, God has seen fit to bless many Christians with more wealth than Christians in many other parts of the world. The church, by virtue of the relative wealth of its members, has access to more capital than at any other time in history.

With these great resources, God is doing great things through technology and the efforts of faithful Christians, yet we believe there is a huge missing opportunity because of a subtle shift in worldview. The way many Christians think about their money is influenced by the world rather than by the Bible.

This has at least a three-fold impact: First, since many believe that money exists for their good and comfort, they seek to gain as much as they can to spend it on their own comforts and enjoyment. This means that Christians become more inward-focused and lose sight of all that God is calling them to in this world. They don't want to get out of their comfort zones to help others or share the gospel.

Second, the result of this kind of selfish thinking causes some Christians to hold on to more of their money than they ought. They fear that generosity may cause them to not have enough for their needs and wants.

Third, many believers never experience the blessing of generosity and living with a Gospel-focused view of their money and resources. Perhaps another way of saying this is that the spiritual development and sanctification of these believers are hindered by their view of money.

Wealth Can Drive Us From God

One of the Puritans, Thomas Brooks (1608-1680), made a comment that deeply resonates with those who want to be a good steward. He said, "Adversity hath slain her thousands, but prosperity her ten thousands." Everyone wants to avoid hardship and lack. I've never heard someone say, "Lord, please don't make me rich." Yet that is exactly what we see in **Proverbs 30:7-9**: "Two things I ask of you; deny them not to me before I die: ... give me neither poverty nor riches; feed me with the food that is needful for me, [9] lest I be full and deny you and say, 'Who is the LORD?' or lest I be poor and steal and profane the name of my God." This passage supports the statement from Brooks that wealth presents us with a unique danger.

Before we look at what the Bible says about the dangers of wealth, we want to be explicit that there are many examples in Scripture of Godly and wealthy people. We are not anti-wealth. That being said, there are clear warnings throughout the Bible for those who have or pursue riches:

Mark 4:19—*But the cares of the world and the deceitfulness of riches and the desires for other things enter in and choke the word, and it proves unfruitful.*

Romans 1:25—*They exchanged the truth about God for a lie, and worshiped and served created things rather than the Creator—who is forever praised. Amen.* (NLT)

1 Timothy 6:17—*As for the rich in this present age, charge them not to be haughty or set their hopes on the uncertainty of riches, but on God who richly provides us everything to enjoy.*

From these verses, we can gather the following:
- When we have wealth, our confidence can begin to shift from God to our money. This causes us to have more trust in our wealth than in the promises of God found in Scripture.
- Everyone worships something or someone. Apart from Christ, the default human condition is to worship anything but God.

Our ultimate allegiance is revealed when we observe our spending habits.

- When we put our trust in our wealth, we are no longer trusting in the never-changing, always faithful God of the universe. Rather, we find more comfort in trusting the shifting sands of our fleeting wealth.

These truths are counter-intuitive to what we've been conditioned to believe about money, and they also make it clear that there's risk involved in entertaining these false beliefs. Really, our financial problems can be boiled down to a single root cause:

We value money more than God—this is the worship problem.

The Worship Problem

Now, when we use the word "worship" in this context, we aren't referring to the two hours spent at church on Sundays. We aren't bowing down to the altar of money. We're saying that when we value money more than God, we have a worship problem. Worship in this context means that money and all that comes with it becomes the controlling desire of hearts. We place faith in our ability to earn, or the value of our portfolios. As soon as we start trusting in our money, it pulls us away from God. We'll never find any lasting hope, peace, strength, or confidence in our money.

Our worship problem is well summarized in **Romans 1:22-23**: *Claiming to be wise, they became fools, and exchanged the glory of the immortal God for images resembling mortal man and birds and animals and creeping things.*

This passage teaches that worshiping the wrong things is a fundamental flaw of every human being. God created and called us to be worshipers, but since the time of Adam, every human being has worshiped anything and everything except God. The problem persists to this day and is present in all of our churches and in each of our hearts.

We know there are many who would argue with this logic, stating they don't believe in God, and therefore worship nothing. But the world is not divided between worshipers and non-worshipers. As

Romans 1 clearly teaches, every single human being worships *something or someone.*

If we don't worship money, it's likely that we worship pleasure, social status, creature comforts, or the "athlete gods" of professional sports. Even seemingly good things like family or our jobs can become idols in our lives if we don't keep them in their proper place. The question begs to be answered: Do we worship God? Or do we worship the things He has created? What about the things we have created? Idols like entertainment, convenience, and technology.

The Solution: Renewing Your Mind

So, what's the solution to this deep, inherent worship problem? It's given to us in **Romans 12:2**: *Do not be conformed to this world, but be transformed by the renewal of your mind, that by testing you may discern what is the will of God, what is good and acceptable and perfect.*

So, how do we transform and renew our minds? How do we reclaim the Biblical way of thinking or worldview? We do this by valuing God's Word above all, and promoting the supremacy of Christ in all things. We allow the Word of God to change our hearts and minds, learn and carry out what the Bible teaches, and invite Christ to take His proper place in our hearts.

When our minds are renewed, the way we value and prioritize money changes. We now want to become even better stewards of all that God has entrusted to our care. Embracing Scripture as the foundation for everything we do is key for our transformational handling of money. In fact, the Bible provides us with an *entire framework* to guide us in financial stewardship! We'll discuss this framework in detail in Chapter 3.

The Stewardship Journey

In this book, we'll take you on a journey to become a better steward. Think of this book as a roadmap for the journey to help you reach your financial goals the way God intended.

We'll begin the journey in Part One by laying the foundation for Biblical stewardship.

- In Chapter One, we'll expand upon the definition of stewardship. You'll learn what stewardship is, what it isn't, and why it's so important in this life.
- In Chapter Two, we'll discuss the importance of priorities, the consequences of misplaced priorities, and why priorities matter to God.
- In Chapter Three, we'll introduce you to the *Five Biblical Financial Priorities*. We'll explain each priority, why each one is significant, and how they fit together to create a complete picture of stewardship.

The journey continues in Part Two, where we'll discuss the call to every generation to become better stewards.

- In Chapter Four, we'll talk about training the next generation to become wise stewards. We'll present proven, hands-on teaching methods and activities that you can incorporate into your children's lives as they learn to manage finances.
- In Chapter Five, we'll discuss the Biblical and real-life implications of loving money and why the love of money is a root of all kinds of evil.
- In Chapter Six, we'll redefine wealth. We'll compare and contrast worldly vs. Biblical uses of wealth, and the importance of being rich toward God.
- In Chapters Seven and Eight, we'll provide an application to the Biblical wisdom discussed thus far. First, in Chapter Seven, we'll address how stewards can properly manage and grow the wealth entrusted to them. Next, we'll talk about how to manage God's wealth as we prepare for retirement in Chapter Eight.

We conclude the journey in Part Three, where we discuss the potential impact your stewardship can have on future generations.

- In Chapter Nine, we'll talk about Estate Planning, the steps you can take to leave a legacy for your family and ministry and how your stewardship can change the world.

- In Chapter Ten, we'll summarize and conclude the book by considering the three dangers and ultimate rewards for good stewardship.

Our hope is that this roadmap gives you encouragement and guides you to take the proper, God-led steps to prepare for your future. Reading this book won't guarantee financial success, but it will help direct your steps, giving you the *best chance* at future success on earth and in heaven. We believe that as you read this book and learn more about stewardship, you will have the knowledge and tools to make the right financial choices according to Scripture. As you grow in this area of your life you'll be on your way to developing good, lifelong habits. And, best of all, your peace and confidence will grow as you learn to trust God with the outcome!

Unexpected Detours

Becoming a good steward may be simple, but it's not *easy*. The journey to stewardship excellence is a long one, and the reality of traveling any long distance is that there will always be unexpected interruptions and delays. We could make wise financial decisions that are in line with God's Word and be making great progress, but a cancer diagnosis, loss of a job, a divorce, or another unexpected event could force us to take a detour. Even something minor like a car repair could throw a wrench in our plans.

The good news is, if you're a good steward, you'll be better prepared to handle these unexpected events. All good stewards know that God is the ultimate provider, and they keep their eyes on Him, especially when things don't go as planned.

When unexpected events happen, we know they are no surprise to God. God has so much in store for us, and He knows what the future holds. So, as we travel on this stewardship journey, we look to God to lead us and show us our next move. As **Proverbs 16:9** says, *"The heart of a man plans his way, but the Lord establishes his steps."*

This means that when the unexpected happens, we put one foot in front of the other trusting in God, and we press on.

Why Listen to Us?

We've given you a preview of what we know about Biblical financial stewardship. At this point, you may be wondering why you should listen to us. Let us briefly introduce ourselves and tell you about our experiences. The first thing you should know is that the authors are father and son. Second, we work together helping Christians make wise choices with their money through our stewardship ministry and financial advising company. Third, like you, we're still on the path toward good stewardship. Being a Good Steward is a lifestyle of seeking to honor God with all that you have. That means that we're in process just like you are. And finally, our primary goal is to help you, our reader, become an even better steward.

Roy Russell

I've been working in financial services since 1978. It has been my privilege to walk with many families as they navigate the many complexities of life. As I reflected on Scripture and how it is applied to our financial lives, it became apparent that Christians often did not have a framework for understanding how to honor God in this area of their lives. I found that our Biblical framework for financial stewardship really helped folks prioritize their spending and savings decisions. My clients' confidence and joy increased as they gave faithfully to their local church, saved for the future, paid their bills on time, looked for ways to bless those who are less fortunate than them, and enjoyed God's rich blessings. Over time, these principles have been refined and developed into our 3-day Stewardship Lifestyle Seminar put on by Life Institute, our ministry arm. If you'd like to learn more about my credentials and background, you can learn more here. https://www.thelifegroup.org/about/staff/

Tim Russell

Financial stewardship has been an important part of my life since I was very young. Today, I get to carry on my family's legacy by leading The Life Financial Group and Life Institute into the next generation. It is a privilege to lead our team of advisors and stewardship teachers as we help fulfill our mission to help Christians become even better stewards of all their assets. As part of our weekly *Stewardology Podcast* (www.StewardologyPodcast.com), I get to develop and teach the intersection of Biblical stewardship and theology.

It's Never Too Late

If you've been making good choices with your money, our hope is that this book provides you with reassurance that you've been doing the right thing and gives you the encouragement to continue.

If you feel that you've been making poor decisions, or you're disappointed, discouraged, or confused, we hope this book will lift you up and help you turn things around. It's never too late to start making positive changes!

The responsibility of stewardship applies to all believers, regardless of your race, ethnicity, gender, age, or marital status. Even your previous mistakes do not disqualify you from the call to good stewardship. This book was written to help you manage your resources while planning for the future so you can hear the affirmation that all good stewards long to hear, "Well done, good and faithful servant."

To reach that destination, we need to trust in God and value what He values. We need to be generous and rich toward God, save, and prepare for the future. This book—this roadmap—will lead and guide you in these things, because as you'll discover, the foundation for this roadmap is God's Word.

Now, let's begin our journey to becoming good stewards of God's resources!

PART 1: THE FOUNDATION OF BIBLICAL STEWARDSHIP

Chapter 1:

An Introduction to Stewardship

Bob is married, has two kids, and a job he enjoys. He works hard, sometimes up to 60 hours a week. When he gets paid, his priorities are to pay the bills and enjoy life. He doesn't really pay close attention to his spending. More often than not, he spends more than he earns, leading to higher and higher credit card bills. The pressure of these bills is mounting and Bob feels like he's losing control of his spending. When money comes up in discussions with his wife, the discussions always end in a fight.

What's going on with Bob is an all too common problem today. He views himself as the ultimate owner of his life—he gets to call the shots and choose how he wants to live. His money is about his enjoyment. Bob doesn't understand that rather than being the ultimate owner of his income and resources, he's the steward or caretaker of all that he has.

As a steward, if Bob is the caretaker, who, then, is the owner?

The secular world would like us to believe that we are the owners of money and possessions. Biblically speaking, this belief misses the mark. The Bible points to God as the ultimate owner of all things. As **Psalm 24:1** says, *"The earth is the LORD's and the fullness thereof, the world and those who dwell therein."* This means that He is the creator, provider, and sustainer of all that was, is, and ever will be. As human beings, we have a very short span of influence over what we are stewards of, but God's span of influence is eternal.

In this chapter, we'll explore the Biblical definition and explanations of stewardship. We'll reference Scripture, but for the scope and purposes of this book, we won't dive deeply into all of the verses cited. We encourage you to study and explore further any and all of the verses to expand your learning and understanding.

What is Stewardship?

Webster's dictionary defines "stewardship" as "the conducting, supervising, or managing of something, especially the careful and responsible management of something entrusted to one's care." While this definition is helpful, it doesn't address the spiritual dimension of stewardship. Perhaps this definition is even more to the point: "stewardship is the responsibility to manage all of the resources of life for the glory of God, acknowledging God as provider." [1]

Notice the difference between ownership and stewardship. An owner has rights while the steward has responsibilities. The steward is responsible for managing the resources or property of the owner. For example, when you let a friend borrow one of your belongings, you have the right to say what your friend can or can't do with your property, right? This is because the item does not belong to your friend–it belongs to you. Likewise, God has the right to determine the best use of the resources entrusted to our care, because He is the owner.

Responsibility of Stewardship
"So, whether you eat or drink, or whatever you do, do all to the glory of God" —1 Corinthians 10:31.

As stewards, we are responsible for achieving the objectives of the Owner. We are to work hard to care for and cultivate God's creation (**Genesis 1:28 & 2:15**). With regard to the time, talents, treasures, and

[1] From Charles W. Draper with Stewart Don H., "Stewardship," ed. Chad Brand et al., Holman Illustrated Bible Dictionary (Nashville, TN: Holman Bible Publishers, 2003), pg 1534.

relationships that God has entrusted to us, we are to act in such a way that will bring glory to God.

Rather than recognizing God's rights as the Creator and owner of the world, however, we assert our perceived rights to do whatever we want with our lives and possessions. This results in our making a mess of the world in which we have stewardship. Consider the story of Adam and Eve. They asserted their perceived rights over the forbidden fruit, resulting in the curse. Their son Cain asserted his rights over his brother Abel, leading to the first murder. We could go on and on with examples of humans asserting their rights and failing to properly care for this world and all that is in it. When we resist the fact that we have a *responsibility* to be stewards of this world according to God's design, we make life miserable for ourselves and those around us.

As a steward, we are the only one responsible to manage or tend what God has entrusted to us. If you've been a poor steward, you can't shift the blame for poor stewardship onto others around you. While the environment in which we were raised and live has a profound impact on how we think about money, our environment is not responsible for our actions.

If you feel shame over past poor stewardship, we have good news for you. First, your past does not define your worth, and it doesn't mean you can't grow in this area of life. You can let go of your feelings of shame, because you don't earn God's favor through your stewardship. If you have struggled with your responsibility to be a wise steward of your resources as a believer, look to Christ. He has suffered the punishment that you deserve for your sins, including the sin of poor stewardship. Second, Jesus is not just a good steward. He is the Great Steward. He takes all of our sin and failure and gives us His perfect obedience and righteousness. Stop looking at your failures and start looking to Christ. Your primary goal is not to become some sort of super steward, but rather to *become more like Him*. Finally, because of the previous two points, change is possible. Our prayer is that this book will be part of your stewardship growth journey.

Accountability of Stewardship

"Moreover, it is required of stewards that they be found faithful"—1 Corinthians 4:2.

If we are responsible to handle our resources in such a way as to accomplish God's plan for His world, then it follows that we will be held accountable for our stewardship. One day, you and I will stand before God and provide an answer for how we handled our time, talents, and treasures.

Consider the parable of the talents found in **Matthew 25:14-30**. In this parable, a master entrusts his property and talents (money) to three servants. The servants did not own the property or the money, but they were responsible for managing it wisely. Two of the servants went out, traded their talents, and doubled their resources. The third servant, out of fear, hid the talent so it would not be lost. After a time, the master returned and inspected his servants. He was pleased with the two servants who had doubled their talents, but he was not pleased with the timid approach of the last servant. The master judged this servant as wicked and lazy, then he took what he had entrusted to this servant and gave it to the first servant, so he could better manage this portion of the money.

The idea of accountability can sound intimidating. It can feel like God's a police officer in the sky, waiting to punish you for poor stewardship. Friend, take heart. Jesus Christ has accomplished all that we could not. If you feel shame or guilt over past stewardship choices, look to Jesus. He stands ready to forgive and walk with you as you grow in your role as a steward.

Reward of Stewardship

"His master said to him, 'Well done, good and faithful servant. You have been faithful over a little; I will set you over much. Enter into the joy of your master"—Matthew 25:21.

Let's break down the major points of this verse from the Parable of the Talents:

1. **"Well done, good and faithful servant"** - These are words every Christian longs to hear. If our goal is to please the Lord,

we must seek to use His resources to advance His purposes. In so doing, we will hear Him say, "well done, good and faithful servant."

2. **"Servant"** - Our relationship to the Lord will not change. We are His servants. He is our master. We don't own anything. He owns it all.

3. **"Faithful over a little"**- No matter how much talent, ability, money, or possessions the Lord entrusts to you, it's still only "a little." God expects you to be responsible for what He's entrusted to you.

4. **"Set you over much"** - God promises rewards for wise stewardship. These may or may not include material or financial rewards, but will always include eternal, spiritual rewards which are far greater. The earthly reward for wise stewardship is often greater responsibility. We have to keep our minds and hearts on the reality that stewardship is all about pleasing the Lord, not to get more stuff.

5. **"Enter into the joy of your master"** - It's one thing to know you please the Lord, but it's an entirely different thing to experience the *good pleasure* of the Lord. When we please God, we experience the pleasure God already has for us. We don't make God love us any more than He already does. Rather, our experience of that love is fuller. Isn't this what heaven is all about? Experiencing God's joy for all eternity? We can take comfort in knowing this promise is not just for the hereafter— it's for right here and right now!

How Does Stewardship Impact Our Thoughts and Actions?

When we truly grasp the Biblical concept of stewardship, we will come to learn that stewardship isn't a to-do list, it is a lifestyle. Our stewardship isn't just about managing our income and possessions; it also includes how we manage our relationships, work, abilities, time, and health.

For example, when we think about our relationships, we should consider what God wants us to do in and through them. How can we glorify God in our interactions with others? When it comes to our work, we should carry it out as if we work for the Lord Jesus Christ—as if He is our boss. Consider **Ephesians 6:5–6**: *"Bondservants, obey your earthly masters... as you would Christ, not by the way of eye-service, as people-pleasers, but as bondservants of Christ, doing the will of God from the heart."*

Don't let the words "bondservant" or "master" distract you from the point Paul is making in these verses. No matter your situation in life, when we see God as the One to whom we owe ultimate allegiance, we can work not only to please our earthly boss, but also to please God.

As we think about our talents and abilities, our goal should not be to use them for the sole advancement of our own good, but for the good of those in the community where the Lord has placed us. We can very well use our talents to earn a living, but we should also use them to benefit those around us. As you can see, stewardship is an all-encompassing reality.

When we understand that God owns everything, our motivation shifts. We no longer use others to get all we can—we begin to use all we have to serve and benefit others.

The further we are from Christlikeness, the more likely we are to use our talents and resources to take advantage of others. However, the more we become like Christ, the more our thoughts and actions will be changed from self-seeking to "others-serving."

Biblical Examples of Stewardship

The Bible is replete with both positive and negative examples of stewardship. Let's explore some of these stories, along with the positive and negative consequences of each one.

Stewardship at Creation

So God created man in his own image, in the image of God he created him; male and female he created them—Genesis 1:27.

Essentially, this verse is saying that man, more than any other created being, reflects the majesty and glory of God. This means that as humans, we have dignity, value, and worth. Our lives have meaning.

Before Adam ate the forbidden fruit in **Genesis 3**, God gave him a job. He was to tend the Garden of Eden. Adam did not own the garden; he was a caretaker, or a steward of it. He had the responsibility to care for it in the same way God would have done.

Sometimes we think that work is bad or something to be avoided. Notice, however, that work (tending the garden, **Genesis 1:28-30)** *precedes* the fall of mankind and the cursing of the ground (the thorns and thistles, **Gen 3:17-19**). In other words, work is part of God's good creation. It's only when sin entered the world that work became frustrating. This not only means that work is good—it's also part of what it means to have been made in the image of God. Without purposeful work, men and women lack meaning in their lives. God created us for work.

Stewardship of Joseph

Joseph is one of the most well-known characters in the Bible. We may be familiar with his story which appears in **Genesis 37-50,** but it's possible for us to miss the important lessons it contains.

In the beginning, Joseph was a teenager. His brothers were jealous of the favor their father Jacob showed him, so they faked his death and sold him into slavery. Potiphar, one of Pharaoh's high-ranking military officials, purchased him. Rather than growing bitter, Joseph worked hard and trusted God. The Lord blessed everything Joseph touched, and he was soon given the responsibility of caring for all of Potiphar's property.

All seemed to be going well until Potiphar's wife tried to seduce Joseph. He refused her advances, and his rejection angered her, so Potiphar's wife wrongfully accused him of seducing *her*. Joseph ended up going to prison.

Joseph's story seems like a yo-yo. There were more peaks and valleys in his life than many of us will ever face. Rather than growing bitter, he trusted that God was in control and was working out His perfect plan.

While Joseph was in prison, Pharaoh sought him and gave him the opportunity to interpret specific dreams he had. From the dreams, Joseph predicted seven years of amazing harvest and seven years of devastating drought. Seeing Joseph's insight, Pharaoh gave him charge over all of Egypt and tasked him with preparing for the drought. Joseph rose to prominence, and his exercise of stewardship not only saved Egypt, but also his family and the nation of Israel. Because of Joseph's stewardship, Jesus was able to come into the world and fulfill God's plan of salvation. From Joseph's story, we gather the following:

1. **The Lord was with Joseph.** Several times in these passages, we read that "the Lord was with Joseph." While it's true that Joseph worked hard and exerted all of his effort to honor the Lord and accomplish his goals, at the end of the day, his efforts could only take him so far. Scripture tells us that unless the Lord builds the house, the builders labor in vain (**Psalm 127:1**). We should recognize our need for the Lord to bless our work.

2. **Success and setbacks often come together.** God blessed His servant Joseph, but He also allowed setbacks to thwart Joseph's plans. When our plans aren't working out as we hoped, it doesn't mean God's plan will fail. God allowed the situation with Potiphar's wife to go badly, but not because He was displeased with Joseph. God needed to place Joseph in the right place for the next stage of his stewardship journey. This means we shouldn't be surprised or frustrated when setbacks come our way—it could be that God is placing us right where He wants us! It may not be apparent what God is doing until after all is said and done. We should trust in the Lord, not in what our eyes can see.

3. **Stewardship responsibilities grow with faithfulness.** Joseph's path to the blessings of God was not a straight line. Each time Joseph had a setback, he proved himself faithful, and the Lord blessed him with more responsibility. Joseph started out as an entitled child with little wisdom. With each setback, he submitted himself to the goodness of God, growing in wisdom and responsibility. Joseph's faithfulness to serve where he was placed eventually brought him to the second highest position in Egypt.

4. **Stewardship has a far-reaching impact.** Joseph's stewardship of Egypt's limited resources had generational impacts. Not only did he preserve the lives of countless Egyptians, but his stewardship also provided for his family from which came the Nation of Israel and the Messiah, Jesus Christ. Stewardship is not just about meeting your personal needs; God uses our stewardship to be part of His grand plan for this world and the advance of His Kingdom.

Stewardship of Solomon

Solomon, one of the great kings of Israel, and perhaps one of the wisest and wealthiest men who ever lived, wrote the Book of Proverbs. The wisdom he shares has everything to do with stewardship, however, we must be careful when approaching the Book of Proverbs, because unlike other parts of the Bible, it does not give universal statements of truth. Rather, the Book of Proverbs is a collection of wise sayings to help the reader live life God's way, and it is full of observations about how God created this world to work.

The following are samples of proverbs which address various aspects of stewardship:

- **Proverbs 10:4-5** - *A slack hand causes poverty, but the hand of the diligent makes rich. He who gathers in summer is a prudent son, but he who sleeps in harvest is a son who brings shame.*
- **Proverbs 11:4** - *Riches do not profit in the day of wrath, but righteousness delivers from death.*
- **Proverbs 14:24** - *The crown of the wise is their wealth, but the folly of fools brings folly.*
- **Proverbs 21:20** - *Precious treasure and oil are in a wise man's dwelling, but a foolish man devours it.*
- **Proverbs 22:3 & 27:12** - *The prudent sees danger and hides himself, but the simple go on and suffer for it.*
- **Proverbs 23:4–5** - *Do not toil to acquire wealth; be discerning enough to desist. When your eyes light on it, it is gone, for suddenly it sprouts wings, flying like an eagle toward heaven.*

- **Proverbs 28:25** - *A greedy man stirs up strife, but the one who trusts in the LORD will be enriched.*
- **Proverbs 28:27** - *Whoever gives to the poor will not want, but he who hides his eyes will get many a curse.*

As you can see, Solomon has a lot to say about stewardship in Proverbs as it relates to work, wealth, planning, and reserves. Several of these verses are referenced and explained in later chapters. Wisdom is not reserved to the Old Testament. The apostle Paul refers to Jesus as "the wisdom of God" (**1 Corinthians 1:24**). Let's now consider what Jesus has to teach us about stewardship.

Stewardship in the Parables of Jesus

In the Bible, Jesus talks about money and possessions more frequently than He does heaven, hell, or prayer. We've already considered His parable of the talents, but there are many other parables where Jesus addresses financial stewardship. Jesus' primary motive in these parables isn't to teach us financial lessons, but to help us understand matters of eternal significance.

The following is a list of several parables that address the topic of stewardship, but to go into detail with each of them, we'd have to write another book. Consider taking some time to read through these passages, and reflect on the teachings of Jesus as they relate to stewardship.

- Parables of the Hidden Treasure and Pearl of Great Price (**Matthew 13:44-45**)
- Parable of the Unforgiving Servant (**Matthew 18:23-25**)
- Parable of the Talents and Ten Minas (**Matthew 25:14-30; Luke 19:11-27**)
- Parable of the Rich Fool (**Luke 12:16-21**)
- Parable of the Prodigal Son (**Luke 15:11-32**)
- Parable of the Shrewd Manager (**Luke 16:1-12**)

Money can have a great impact on our heart. With it, we can bless others and worship God, or we can hoard or spend it, leading to our ruin. However, Jesus is more powerful than the devastating impacts of sinful uses of money. Just as in the parable of the prodigal son, Jesus can redeem our failures and mistakes with money.

The Cost and Opportunity of Stewardship

Having discussed the concept of stewardship in this chapter, we thought it would be wise to close with a sober acknowledgement that being a good steward isn't an easy job. It involves giving up our perceived "rights" to all that we have, and submitting to God's will. These words are easy to say, but hard to live out. We, the authors of this book, will never claim to be perfect stewards. We struggle with our perceived rights, too.

Being a good steward doesn't mean you will have riches. While being a good steward means you recognize that this life is not all there is, you acknowledge the fact that this life is the only opportunity you have to impact the life to come—life with God in heaven for all eternity. Those who are good stewards make it a priority to properly care for that which has been entrusted to them, while investing their time and resources in ministries and activities that have eternal value.

The Cost of Stewardship, essentially, is giving up the right to spend your money on your own desires. The Reward of Stewardship is pleasing our Heavenly Father and our eternal joy in Heaven. As missionary Jim Elliot wrote in his personal journal prior to giving up his life to reach a remote tribe, "He is no fool who gives up what he cannot keep to gain that which he cannot lose."

Chapter 2:

The Context of Stewardship

Introduction to Haggai: The Danger of Misplaced Priorities

If you were to go to the emergency room with a gunshot wound, and the doctor notices that you happen to also have an ingrown toenail, you'd be outraged if the ER doctor treated your ingrown toenail first, right? Failure to prioritize the gunshot wound would be fatal to you and to the doctor's career!

The above scenario illustrates the importance of recognizing priorities. We face the challenge of identifying right priorities on earth, and also in the spiritual realm. To discuss the reality of this challenge (and what could happen if we fail), let's talk about what happened to God's people in the book of Haggai when they chose to place their focus on the wrong priorities.

Where Does Haggai Fall in Redemptive History?

God established Israel as a nation to demonstrate His glory and wisdom to the world, but they rebelled against His gracious rule and followed after other gods. Not allowing their sin and rebellion to go unaddressed, God sent Babylon to remind Israel of their dependence upon Him. Babylon's invasion resulted in the destruction of Jerusalem in 586 BC. The Temple and the city walls lay in ruin and the Babylonians marched the Israelites into exile.

The Persian king, Cyrus the Great, captured Babylon in 539 BC and allowed Israel to return to Jerusalem the following year. Cyrus wrote an edict instructing Israel to rebuild the Temple of God (**Ezra 1**). Israel started out well, but they stopped short of rebuilding the Temple. After completing the walls of Jerusalem and the Temple foundation, the nation became distracted with day-to-day frustrations and challenges.

What Was the Big Deal About the Temple Anyway?

Why was the Temple so important to God? The Temple was not just symbolically important to Israel, it was critically important to the spiritual health and vitality of the community. Only in the Temple could the Israelites perform the ritual sacrifices as commanded by the Law. Without the Temple, the people would be adrift spiritually. Israel's failure to build the Temple demonstrated their lack of desire for God.

Furthermore, we see that the rebuilding of the Temple points to the establishment of the Church, the indwelling of the Holy Spirit (**1 Corinthians 3:16 & Ephesians 2:20-22**), and ultimately the New Jerusalem (**Revelation 21:9-11:5**). God ordained the Temple to be rebuilt so that His plan for mankind could be carried out. We know from history that this Temple ultimately failed to help the nation of Israel remain faithful to God. It was destroyed in 70 AD along with all of Jerusalem. But while Jesus was on earth, the Temple played a central role in His life and death.

The events of Haggai 1 take place in the year 520 BC. This chapter is divided into three parts, and we'll discuss each part individually.

Part One: Israel's Misplaced Priorities Exposed

Without the Temple, the nation was spiritually adrift, which led to disastrous results. They were facing significant challenges and difficulties. This is when God sent His prophet, Haggai, to deliver this message to Israel:

2)Thus says the LORD of hosts: 'These people say the time has not yet come to rebuild the house of the LORD.' 3) Then the word of the LORD came by the hand of Haggai the prophet, 4) 'Is it a time for you yourselves to dwell in your paneled houses, while this house lies in ruins?' 5) Now, therefore, thus says the LORD of hosts: 'Consider your ways. 6) You have sown much, and harvested little. You eat, but you never have enough; you drink, but you never have your fill. You clothe yourselves, but no one is warm. And he who earns wages does so to put them into a bag with holes.'"
(Haggai 1:2-6)

Israel's Excuse

One of the first tasks the nation of Israel was to complete upon their return was to rebuild the Temple. They started off strong, but the work eventually came to a halt. Why did the work stop? Israel had plenty of excuses. Verse 2 boils all of their excuses down to this:

"God, the timing is just not right."

It's not as though Israel wanted to disobey; they just kept running into problems. There had been economic hardship, financial strain, and even hostility from the local population. Look at the difficulties Israel was experiencing (vs 6):

- Crop Failure: "You have sown much, and harvested little."
- Food Insecurity: "You eat, but you never have enough;"
- Drought: "You drink, but you never have your fill."
- Sickness and Disease: "You clothe yourselves, but no one is warm."
- Financial Distress: "And he who earns wages does so to put them into a bag with holes."

Let's be honest, this is a list of incredible challenges. While it doesn't excuse Israel's choice to disobey God, it does help us understand just how difficult things were. When it comes to your life, are you dealing with any of the challenges Israel faced? Do you find yourself making excuses to justify your stewardship choices?

God's Perspective

God wanted Israel to see things from His point of view. He sent Haggai to ask them, "Is it a time for you to be living in paneled houses while the Temple remains a ruin?" (v. 4). Israel had many excuses for why they couldn't finish rebuilding the Temple, but they had managed to find the time, money, and resources to fix up their own homes. Clearly, their priorities were not God's priorities!

The people of Israel may have been able to fool each other, but they could not fool God. He knows the secret desires of every heart. Money is a great barometer for what we love and value most, as how we spend money reveals the idols of the human heart. In Israel's case, they valued their own comforts above obeying God.

The book of Haggai is an example of God's way of drawing attention to Israel's sin. You and I, just like Israel, typically respond to Divine confrontation in one of three ways: First, we can ignore it and pretend that everything is normal. Second, we can respond in fear, bracing ourselves for the discipline of God. Or third, we can repent of our sin and move toward God, seeking His forgiving grace, and with His power, live a life pleasing to Him.

The Lord wanted Israel to turn toward Him in repentance. Haggai wants his audience to understand that God is graciously coming to them, not to crush them, but to bring them back into a faithful relationship with Him. It is out of love that God reveals our sin and brokenness. The proper responses to God when He does this are gratitude and obedience.

The bottom line is: Our actions expose where our real priorities lie, because they expose how much we really value God, His Word, our families, our work, our church community, and our own comforts. *Israel's priorities were not God's priorities.* It's not what we say, but what we *do* that exposes our real priorities.

Part Two: The Cost of Misplaced Priorities

God doesn't let Israel come to the wrong conclusion about why they are facing difficulties. He wants them to know that He's behind it all—not to break them, but to restore them. He knows that without the Temple as the center of Jewish religious life, they would soon fall back into the same habits and practices which led to their exile in the first place.

7) "Thus says the LORD of hosts: 'Consider your ways. 8) Go up to the hills and bring wood and build the house, that I may take pleasure in it and that I may be glorified, says the LORD. 9) You looked for much, and behold, it came to little. And when you brought it home, I blew it away. Why? declares the LORD of hosts. Because of my house that lies in ruins, while each of you busies himself with his own house. 10) Therefore the heavens above you have withheld the dew, and the earth has withheld its produce. 11) And I have called for a drought on the land and the hills, on the grain, the new wine, the oil, on what the ground brings forth, on man and beast, and on all their labors' (**Haggai 1:7-11**).

The Real Cause of Israel's Struggles

Israel thought they could refuse to obey God's command to rebuild the Temple because of all the struggles they had. In reality, they had it backwards. They were struggling because they put their desire for creature comforts above obeying God.

> *"You looked for much, and behold, it came to little. And when you brought it home, I blew it away"* (vs 9).

There are two important points to realize here: First, the people of God presumed upon the grace of God. Sure, their national sin caused the Babylonian exile, but God had forgiven them and returned them to the Promised Land. Israel probably thought the long-awaited Messiah was just around the corner. They expected God to make them a "great nation" (**Genesis 12:2**) and that He would be "an enemy to [their] enemies and an adversary to [their] adversaries" (**Exodus 23:22**). Once the Messiah showed up, they would finally have payback on the nations that oppressed them. However, they presumed upon the goodness of God by thinking their personal obedience was unimportant.

Second, God is the One who causes Israel's hardships. He says, "I blew it away." God had indeed promised good things for Israel, but they don't come automatically. God calls His children to obedience and faith. When His children stray from following Him with all of their heart, the most loving thing God can do is get their attention. There are two ways in which God gets the attention of His children: He causes hardships that force His children to turn to Him for help, and

He gives them His Word to call them to repentance. In Haggai's day, he brought God's message to Israel. But today, we have the entire Bible in which God speaks to us.

To get Israel's attention, God brought them scarcity, loss, drought, weak harvest, and frustration. These difficulties were the cost of their misplaced priorities. God used difficulty and struggle to get their attention. At times, He may do the same for us. He wasn't trying to crush Israel; He wanted to draw them back into fellowship with Him. He loved them too much to let them live with the consequences of their misplaced priorities.

The Importance of Self-Reflection

The hardships of life are not simply to be endured. God doesn't want His children to have a "stiff upper lip" and press through difficulties. There are several reasons why God would bring hardships into the lives of His children.

First, hardships remind us of our dependence on God for all that we have. When things are going well, we can become proud and convinced that we are self-sufficient. Hardships have a way of humbling us and pointing us to our need for God. Second, hardships build our faith. It is often in the hard times that we feel closest to God. Finally, and specific to this text, hardships are one thing that God uses to lovingly correct His sinful children. So how do we know what God is doing in our lives through hardship? God gives us the answer to the question of what He's doing in verses 5 and 7 of our text.

"Now, therefore, thus says the LORD of hosts: **Consider your ways***"* (vs 5, emphasis added).

"Thus says the LORD of hosts: **Consider your ways***"* (vs 7, emphasis added).

Twice God says, "Consider your ways." He placed great emphasis on the importance of self-reflection. He wanted the Israelites to pause and consider how they were living. They were to evaluate the condition of their heart. The constant hardships God's Chosen faced gave them the perfect opportunity to consider if there was a sin issue that God wanted to bring to their attention. From our vantage point, with the aid of Scripture, we know that Israel's suffering was caused by their sin.

Hardships are not brought into our lives to crush us, but to point us to God. It is not out of anger or wrath that God brings difficulties into the lives of His children. Consider **Hebrews 12**:

> *5)And have you forgotten the exhortation that addresses you as sons? 'My son, do not regard lightly the discipline of the Lord, nor be weary when reproved by him. 6) For the* **Lord disciplines the one he loves, and chastises every son whom he receives.'** *7) It is for discipline that you have to endure. God is treating you as sons. For what son is there whom his father does not discipline? 9) Besides this, we have had earthly fathers who disciplined us and we respected them. Shall we not much more be subject to the Father of spirits and live? 10) For they disciplined us for a short time as it seemed best to them,* **but he disciplines us for our good, that we may share his holiness.** *11) For the moment all discipline seems painful rather than pleasant, but later* **it yields the peaceful fruit of righteousness** *to those who have been trained by it* (**Hebrews 12:5–11**, emphasis added).

As Christians, hardships should be encouraging because they tell us that God loves us and wants to create holiness and Christlikeness within us. Hardships are not punishment for sin; Jesus bore the full weight of God's wrath for our sin on the Cross. You and I will never be punished for that which Jesus has already been punished. However, our Heavenly Father does discipline His children to build a godly character in them, resulting in peace and righteousness. If you are facing difficulty in your life, slow down, reflect on your walk with God, and evaluate what God might be trying to teach you through the hardship.

However, we want to be careful and avoid two extremes when it comes to hardship. We don't want to be like Job's friends (who were wrong) when they said Job's suffering indicated or proved that Job was a wicked man. But we also don't want to ignore texts like Haggai 1, which show us that God uses suffering to reveal sin.

So, how should we respond if we sense that God is dealing with us and our sin? Turn to God! Consider **James 4:6-7a & 10**:

> [6] *But he gives more grace. Therefore it says, 'God opposes the proud but gives grace to the humble.'* [7] ***Submit** yourselves therefore to God…* [10] ***Humble** yourselves before the Lord, and he will exalt you.* (**James 4:6-7a, 10,** emphasis added)

As we humble ourselves before God, admitting our sin and seeking His grace, this text says that God 'gives more grace.' His grace is more than enough to forgive our sins and restore us to a right relationship with Him. It's grace upon grace (**John 1:16**).

One final warning before we move on to the next idea in this text is: God calls us to "self" reflection. When we see suffering in the lives of those around us, let's not jump to the conclusion that God is addressing some form of sin in their lives. God says "consider *your* ways," not your neighbors' ways. When we have knowledge that our priorities are not in line with God's, we need to spend time in reflection and prayer. We should ask God to reveal and expose areas of sin in our lives to His unchanging grace, so that He can change *us*. God is more than able to do this sanctifying work in our lives.

Part Three: Hope for All With Misplaced Priorities

We've established that God does not bring difficulty into the lives of Christians to crush or destroy us. He uses these trials so we will return and restore our relationships with Him. Israel came to this realization, and their reaction displayed true repentance:

> [12] *Then… all the remnant of the people, obeyed the voice of the Lord their God, and the words of Haggai the prophet, as the Lord their God had sent him. And the people feared the Lord.* [13] *Then Haggai, the messenger of the Lord, spoke to the people with the Lord's message, "I am with you, declares the Lord."* [14] *And the Lord stirred up the spirit of Zerubbabel the son of Shealtiel, governor of Judah, and the spirit of Joshua the son of Jehozadak, the high priest, and the spirit of all the remnant of the people. And they came and worked on the house of the Lord of hosts, their God.* **(Haggai 1:12-14)**

Hope Found in Repentance

As you consider the situation of Israel and God's correction of them, you might be feeling discouraged. Some people think of God like the "great police officer in the sky" just looking for people who've stepped out of line so that He can slap the law down on them. Israel sinned, failed to adopt God's priorities, and they reaped the consequences. You may be wondering, is there any hope for Israel or for you and me?

The answer is a resounding "YES!" There is hope for the repentant sinner.

Let's examine the steps of Israel's repentance. First, as the nation grappled with God's message, they came to the realization that they had been living with their priorities out of alignment with God's priorities. They realized that they valued their creature comforts above God's call to rebuild His Temple.

Second, Israel developed a healthy fear of God. **Proverbs 9:10** teaches us that "the fear of the Lord is the beginning of wisdom." This fear is not simply fear of punishment or negative consequences; it is a healthy respect and reverence for the Holiness of God.

Third, Israel obeyed God. They did not allow themselves to be paralyzed by fear, guilt, or shame. They moved toward God by doing what He called them to do. The text tells us that they went out and collected all they needed to complete the Temple. This was not only an act of obedience, but also an act of faith. Remember, they were still facing scarcity, drought, inadequate harvest, and financial frustration. They needed to trust God to provide. Also, notice that this trust was not passive—they went out to gather the supplies and then they "came and worked" on the house of the Lord.

Hope Based on God's Promise

"I am with you, declares the Lord." (verse 13)

Sometimes, we think that we need to get ourselves cleaned up before God will accept us. We think that since we made the mess, we should be the ones to clean it up. This misses the point of God's grace.

God knows that you and I are incapable of cleaning ourselves up, and He does two things to help us in our repentance.

First, God gives us His precious promise, "I am with you, declares the Lord." God does not leave us to wallow in our sin and self-pity. He comes to us. His presence helps us draw out of ourselves and see things from His perspective. This promise to be "with" us is also a promise to be "for" us. **Romans 8:31b-32** tells us about this promise:

> *31) If God is for us, who can be against us? 32) He who did not spare his own Son but gave him up for us all, how will he not also with him graciously give us all things?*

Pause and feel the weight of that last verse. As Christians, God our Father is so committed to our holiness that He sent His Son, Jesus Christ, to suffer the punishment for our sins. Since God would go to such lengths to purchase our salvation, how much more will He provide for our needs? Let us rejoice in God's promise to be "with us!"

"The Lord stirred up the spirit of [the people]" (**verse 14**)

The second thing that God does to help in our repentance is move our hearts to feel our need for Him. God doesn't expose our sin to us and then hope we turn to Him. God is the One who moves our hearts. How gracious God is! He brings about affection, remorse, and true repentance.

We should not assume that Israel's obedience caused God to give this promise. His promise to be with Israel was evidenced by His stirring the hearts of His people. The phrase "stirred up the spirit" indicates that Israel was moved by the grace and forgiveness of the Lord, and they were thankful to still have the privilege of serving the King of Kings. The people responded to God's promise and the stirring up of their spirit with joyful, energetic obedience. God even helped them complete the task He had set before them.

Application of Stewardship

So, what does Haggai 1 have to do with Biblical Stewardship?

First, *the way we spend our money and resources indicates our true priorities.* This is because we spend money on what we love and value the most. Israel spent much of their time, energy, and resources on building comfortable homes for themselves. They did this in spite of the call from God to rebuild His Temple. This reveals that they valued their own comfort over proper worship of God. Today, we can face the same struggle when we invest our time, energy, and resources in our own entertainment and pleasure rather than in the Kingdom of God. We are not saying that entertainment is wrong in and of itself; rather, we are saying that our priorities are out of order when we seek ultimate satisfaction from entertainment instead of from God.

Second, *sometimes God allows financial difficulties to occur in our lives as a way of getting our attention.* When we live our lives in pursuit of our own joy and happiness apart from God, we fail to attain true joy and happiness.

Third, *God enables us to do that which He calls us to do.* Israel was facing all kinds of economic struggles. Could they afford to do what God called them to do? Clearly, the answer was "YES." We can be encouraged by this. If God calls you to do something, you can trust that He will provide all you need to do it. Don't wait for the situations and conditions of your life to be perfect before obeying God's call on your life. Praise God that He has not left us to walk this journey alone; He has provided us with His Word as a guide.

As we come to the end of this chapter, we would like you to evaluate your life's priorities. Do they line up with what God has laid out in Scripture? If they don't, turn to Christ and seek His wisdom to live a life that is consistent with God's Word. Perhaps your current financial struggles are because God is trying to get your attention. He loves you and wants you to redirect your thinking and actions. He wants to bring about a change in your life that aligns with Him and His priorities. There is hope for those with misplaced priorities, and He wants something much better for your life!

In the next chapter, we will introduce the *Five Biblical Financial Priorities of Stewardship* to consider what God says about them and how following them can give you direction and hope in your lives.

Chapter 3:

The Five Biblical Financial Priorities of Stewardship

Now that you understand the definition of stewardship and the consequences of misplaced priorities, let's examine financial priorities as Scripture teaches them and learn how to apply them in your lives.

In many ways, this is the most important chapter of the book because it represents some of the foundational concepts that we use to help Christians become even better stewards of their assets. Understanding and applying these principles is what the rest of the book is all about.

With the Bible as your source and guide, you can learn and apply the five *Biblical Financial Priorities of Stewardship*. In this chapter, we'll introduce you to timeless truths that can help you develop a framework to manage all of God's resources. While we recognize that your financial behaviors should follow certain priorities (for example, paying the mortgage is more important than getting a daily latte), we also realize these behaviors are simultaneous and continuous as you budget, build your savings, and pay the utility bill each month. When properly applied, these financial priorities will fall in line with Scripture, which can dramatically impact your lives.

The Five Priorities

The order of the Five Biblical Financial Priorities corresponds to the order of priorities God has set for us while we're on this earth. Here they are with their corresponding Biblical principles:

Biblical Priority		Corresponding Financial Priority
#1 - God	Therefore ⇒	#1 - Give
#2 - Family	Therefore ⇒	#2 - Save
#3 - Testimony to the World	Therefore ⇒	#3 - Spend
#4 - Less Fortunate	Therefore ⇒	#4 - Offerings
#5 - Ourselves	Therefore ⇒	#5 - Luxuries

- Because God is our highest priority, we give Him back a portion of our income (give).
- Because family is foundational to God's plan for this world, we should save to prepare for the future and avoid debt (save).
- Because God wants our life choices to bring glory to Him, we are to be timely and honorable with our creditors (spend).
- Because God cares about the needs of the poor, we should set aside a portion of our income to be generous toward others (offerings).
- Because God is kind and gracious, we should enjoy God and His blessings (luxuries).

How do you live out the five financial priorities? There are two major ways you use these principles. First, these principles are helpful in making spending decisions. When you understand that God comes first in your lives and that you have limited income, you may choose to forgo spending on a luxury in order to give. Second, you can use these principles when you create your monthly budget. When you sit down each month and plan your spending for the month ahead, you can better visualize these priorities when you list your expenses in the order listed above.

A word of caution before you move forward: what we are presenting in this chapter is not a legalistic framework to judge your own (or others') relationship with God. We don't want to imply that living according to these principles will earn God's favor or avoid His displeasure. These principles are designed to point us to Christ. The only way you and I will ever be able to apply these principles consistently is through the grace of God. As we walk through the rest of this chapter and even the rest of this book, keep your eyes on Christ. As we live out these principles, the goal is that we become more and more like Him.

Give

"Honor the Lord with your wealth and with the firstfruits of all your produce" —Proverbs 3:9.

Why should we give? There are several answers to this question.

Reason 1: We Give Because God Gave.

When we give, we become more like our Heavenly Father. In **John 3:16**, we read, *"For God so loved the world, that he gave..."* Consider what it means that God gave His one and only Son. It was not a tithe; it was not a mere 10 percent. No, God gave His best and most precious gift. He gave us the life of His Son as a sacrifice for our sins. He paid the debt that we could not pay so we could have the life we could never earn, both now and for eternity.

Let's take this line of thinking one step further. If God would go through such pain to secure our salvation, what else is He willing to provide for us? Pause and meditate again on **Romans 8:32**, *"He who did not spare his own Son but gave him up for us all, how will he not also with him graciously give us all things?"* (emphasis added). In the context of this verse, the "all things" that Paul refers to is anything that we might need to withstand the attacks of Satan and fully know the love of God. Wow!

This means that we are secure and fully supplied with all that we will ever need.

Matthew 7:11 is also an interesting text about giving. Here, Jesus reminds us that the goodness of our earthly fathers is a dim reflection of the goodness and generosity of our Heavenly Father: *"If you then, who are evil, know how to give good gifts to your children, how much more will your Father who is in heaven give good things to those who ask Him!"* This truth leads us to the next reason for giving.

Reason 2: We Give Out of Gratitude.

When we see all that God provides for us, our hearts should swell with gratitude, leading us to give back to God. Paul reminds the church of Corinth of this truth in **2 Corinthians 9:7**, *"Each one must give as he has decided in his heart, not reluctantly or under compulsion, for God loves a cheerful giver."*

Likewise, he reminds Timothy in **1 Timothy 6:17-18**, *"as for the rich in this present age, charge them not to be haughty, nor to set their hopes on the uncertainty of riches, but on God, who richly provides us with everything to enjoy. They are to do good, to be rich in good works, to be generous and ready to share."* Notice that generosity and sharing are motivated by gratitude to God who "richly provides us with everything to enjoy."

Reason 3: Giving breaks the power of money in our lives.

This is a truth that was driven home to us by Ron Blue, a thought-leader on Biblical Financial Stewardship and the founder of Kingdom Advisors®. Solomon, perhaps the richest man who ever lived, said in **Ecclesiastes 5:10**, *"He who loves money will not be satisfied with money, nor he who loves wealth with his income."* Solomon understood that the more we have, the more we want. He then explains that giving is a powerful antidote for money's power over us. In **Proverbs 11:24**, he says, *"One gives freely, yet grows all the richer; another withholds what he should give, and only suffers want."*

Also, consider Jesus' words to the rich young ruler found in **Matthew 19:21–22**, *"Jesus said to him, '... go, sell what you possess and give to the poor, and you will have treasure in heaven; and come, follow me.' When the young man heard this he went away sorrowful, for he had great possessions."* This young man was possessed by his possessions, and Jesus knew that giving would break the power of money and possessions in this man's life.

Finally, let's recall Jesus' words in **Matthew 6**. Jesus commands us to lay up for ourselves *"treasures in heaven"* (vs 20). He then goes on to say that *"…where your treasure is, there your heart will be also"* (vs 21). The message is clear: Our heart follows our money. Giving helps us focus our hearts on matters of eternal significance. If we spend a significant portion of our income on temporal things, then our hearts will be focused on those temporal things.

Reason 4: Giving is an act of obedience.

Proverbs 3:9 says, *"Honor the Lord with your wealth and with the firstfruits of all your produce."* The word "honor" is a command for us to use our wealth for His glory, not our own. "Firstfruits" takes this concept of honoring even further as it explicitly brings to mind the offering of firstfruits that God commanded of the nation of Israel in **Deuteronomy 26:2-4**.

In the Old Testament, giving as part of the regular sacrificial system was required. God commanded in **Deuteronomy 16:17** that *"Every man shall give as he is able, according to the blessing of the Lord your God that he has given you."* Later, in **Malachi 3**, the prophet Malachi speaks for God, calling the nation's lack of giving "theft". However, it's interesting that in **Malachi 3:10**, the charge to give is followed by a promise of blessing. *"Bring the full tithe into the storehouse… And thereby put me to the test, says the Lord of hosts, if I will not open the windows of heaven for you and pour down for you a blessing until there is no more need."*

In the New Testament, the concept of giving is further commanded. Let's consider two passages that we've already examined in this chapter: The first is **Matthew 6:20**, where Jesus commands us to "lay up" treasures in heaven. The second passage is **2 Corinthians 9:7**. Paul commands the church in Corinth that *"each one must give as he has decided in his heart."* Generosity and giving are not optional for the believer.

Reason 5: Giving is an act of worship.

1 Timothy 6:9-10 teaches that money can be a cruel taskmaster. In contrast, **Ephesians 4:28** teaches that it can be a wonderful tool. In the Sermon on the Mount, Jesus says, *"No one can serve two masters, for either he will hate the one and love the other, or he will be devoted to the one and despise the other. You cannot serve God and money"* (**Matthew 6:24**). When we give to God, we are saying (to ourselves, to God, and to the world) that God means more to us than money. We proclaim that we truly trust in God, and not in our money. We place our lives and our futures in the gracious hand of God when we give a portion of our income to the church.

How Much Should We Give?

The question of how much of our income we should give as Christians is a challenging one. Some think that since we are under grace, we shouldn't have to give anything. "After all," they think, "God owns the cattle on a thousand hills. He doesn't need my money." Others fear that giving less than ten percent of their gross income will result in God's displeasure or wrath. Both of these ways of thinking are wrong.

In our five-part stewardship framework, giving comes first. We encourage everyone to start by giving ten percent of their income and grow from there.

Tithing versus Grace Giving

You may have noticed that thus far in the book, we've used the word "giving" when referring to what believers ought to do today. We do not object to using the word "tithe," but the word may cause us to miss the amazing truths found in the New Testament about grace giving.

The word "tithe" refers to one-tenth or ten percent. In the Old Testament, the concept of giving a tithe was first introduced when Abraham gave a tenth to Melchizedek (a prefigure of Christ) in **Genesis 14:20**. Later, in **Genesis 28:22**, Jacob promises to give a tithe back to God from all that God provides for him. When God gave Israel the law in **Leviticus 27:30-33**, He required a tenth of their harvest every year.

There were actually three different tithes in the Old Testament.

- 10% for the operation of the Temple and support of the Levites **(Numbers 18: 21, 24)**.
- 10% for the annual feasts and festivals **(Deuteronomy 14:22-27)**.
- 10% for the poor (widows, orphans, and sojourners) every three years **(Deuteronomy 14:28, 29)**.

So, if we do the math correctly, we'd be giving away about 23.3% of our income each year if we followed the Old Testament ways of giving.

Fortunately, in the New Testament, giving shifts from a rigid tithe system to a more open-ended, grace giving model. This doesn't mean that we don't need to give, or that we should keep more of our income. Grace giving is not based on an obligatory 10%; rather, it is our response to God's gracious and abundant provision.

Let's reexamine a verse that we have already considered. In **2 Corinthians 9:7**, Paul says, *"Each one must give as he has decided in his heart, not reluctantly or under compulsion."* Paul does not prescribe that we give 10% of our income. In the New Testament, giving is no longer a matter of the Law—it's a matter of the heart. Each Christian is to consider God's grace in their life and decide how much they ought to give.

In **Luke 6:38**, we learn that our giving impacts our reward: *"Give, and it will be given to you. Good measure, pressed down, shaken together, running over, will be put into your lap. For with the measure you use it will be measured back to you."* Rather than focusing on a percentage, grace giving focuses on the privilege of giving, and the reward for the willing and eager giver.

Author Randy Alcorn teaches that tithes are the training wheels for grace giving. "Tithing isn't the ceiling of giving; it's the floor. It's not the finish line of giving; it's the starting block. Tithes can launch us into the mindset, skills, and habits of grace giving."[2] The idea is not that

---

[2] Alcorn, Randy., The Treasure Principle, Revised and Updated: Unlocking the Secret of Joyful Giving. New York: Multnomah Publishers, 2017

tithing no longer matters in the New Testament, but that we are now free to give *even more*.

Gross versus Net Income

Should you tithe or give based on your gross income (before taxes and deductions), or on your net income (what's left after taxes and deductions)? While it's good to be concerned that selfish motives may influence you to give only what's left over after taxes, insurance, and retirement savings, the question of "gross versus net" misses the point of giving.

As we have just explained, we no longer have an obligation to give a specific percentage. Therefore, we don't give to impress God or others. We give out of gratitude and love for God. In this way, our giving should be so generous that the question of gross versus net is meaningless. No more squabbling over where to put the decimal point. Just give!

Basics of Giving

Now that we've covered our reasons for giving and understand the concept of grace giving, there are a few more important points to address. We have already stated that Christians should seek to start their giving at about 10 percent of their income. But to whom or what should we give these funds?

Giving Basic #1 - Giving to your Local Church.

This first point may seem obvious: you should give to your local church. But why? You give to your local church because God has called that church to preach and teach the Word to you. Your pastors have a responsibility before God to lead, feed, and spiritually protect your family. They are the ones who answer the phone at 2 a.m. when disaster strikes. It is the local church that shares the gospel and encourages your community.

Giving to your local church does not include giving to other worthy non-profit organizations. We have met with Christians who believe they can give $50 a week to their local church and hundreds of dollars to other ministries. While you should give to other ministries as you are able, these funds should not come from the money that you have reserved for the local church.

Giving Basic #2 - Giving to the General Fund.

Rather than designating your giving to "missions" or a "building fund," we encourage believers to give to their local church's general fund. This is because the general fund covers the core functions of the body of Christ. You are free to give to missions, but that falls under the fourth Biblical stewardship principle of "offerings," which we will discuss in detail later in this chapter.

Giving Basic #3 - Giving should be regular.

How often should you give? You should give regularly and consistently. If you get paid weekly, consider giving weekly. This can become a regular part of your worship pattern. If your income fluctuates, consider monthly giving based on the prior month's income. Do not wait until the end of the year to do your giving, as it's more likely you will be tempted to give less out of fear that you won't have enough money for future needs. Also, when you give throughout the year, it's likely you will limit your extra spending to keep it in line with your commitment to give.

Setting up a systematic giving plan through direct deposit, your church's electronic applications, or through online billpay is a great way to make sure your giving is consistent. Make sure you continually review and update your giving as your income changes. We recommend that you conduct an annual review to ensure your giving reflects your current income and ability to give.

Giving Basic #4 - Giving should be anonymous and have no strings attached.

The Good Steward gives with no strings attached. We don't give to manipulate others or for our giving to be seen by others. The Good Steward's primary goal is to honor God who has given us everything, and to contribute funds for your local church's Gospel ministry.

When we say giving should be anonymous, we don't mean that you should only give cash or through completely anonymous means. We mean you shouldn't give primarily to receive the praise of man. As content from the rest of the book will prove, we are in favor of taking tax deductions when they are offered. Anonymous giving does not mean that you shouldn't seek to legally reduce your tax liability. Just don't do your giving primarily for a tax benefit. Someday those tax benefits may be taken away.

Misconceptions About Giving

While the obvious truth is that we give to honor God, unfortunately, there are many misconceptions and ulterior motives when it comes to giving, and we'd like to address those right now. As you read, examine the condition of your heart, and see if you have been believing any of these misconceptions.

Misconception 1: Give to Earn Favor with God

As a Christian, there is no amount of money you could give that would make God love you more than He already does. You are loved and accepted by God just as you are. You can't give your way into Heaven. That being said, *not* giving could be a sign that you love your money more than God.

The truth: *God's love for you is not based upon your giving.*

Misconception 2: Give to Get Rich

The Bible clearly teaches that there is a connection between our giving and God's blessing. We have already looked at a few of these passages. How does that connection between generosity and blessing work? If I want a promotion or a new Rolls Royce, can I just give a large donation to the church, or some TV "evangelist" and God will give me what I want?

The passages in the Bible that show a connection between giving and blessing are real promises. The catch is that we have no say over the timing and manner of how God chooses to distribute His blessings. It may or may not be in this life, but it certainly will be in the life to come.

God is not a cosmic vending machine! He doesn't operate that way. We can't manipulate Him—there's no magic combination of money and button pushing to try to get what you want.

The truth: *We don't give to manipulate God, and we don't give because we expect something in return.*

Misconception 3: Give to Avoid Punishment

Another misconception is that God is a police officer in the sky, watching and monitoring how much every person is giving. God is not waiting around for someone to give less than a certain percentage so He can punish them.

In Jesus' day, the Pharisees were known for being so eager to keep the law that they would tithe on tiny gleanings, like spices. Attention to detail is a good thing to a point, but we shouldn't spend so much time tracking our giving that we neglect the more important spiritual "*matters of the law: justice and mercy and faithfulness*" (**Matthew 23:23**).

The truth: *We serve a God who is loving and full of grace. We don't give out of fear of punishment.*

Misconception 4: Give to Atone for Our Sin

If you have a guilty conscience, you can't give your way out of trouble. Giving does not undo wrong choices. If you have sinned against God, there is no grand gesture of giving that will appease Him. Consider King David's prayer in **Psalm 51:16–17**, "*For you will not delight in sacrifice, or I would give it; you will not be pleased with a burnt offering. The sacrifices of God are a broken spirit; a broken and contrite heart, O God, you will not despise.*"

The truth: *Tithing does not atone for sin. Repentance and turning to God is what He requires.*

Misconception 5: Small Gifts Don't Matter

Some feel that since they don't make much money, they don't need to give. After all, 10 percent of nothing is nothing, right? When Jesus was at the Temple, He observed rich people making a grand spectacle of their great gifts. Then there was a poor widow who put in two coins that were hardly worth counting compared to the other gifts. Jesus remarks that she gave more than the others because she gave out of her poverty, while they gave out of their wealth (**Mark 12:41-44**). The widow's gift was great not because of its size, but because of the faith and love that the gift represents. Her reward will be significant in heaven!

The truth: *Small gifts are significant to God because of the faith and love that those gifts represent.*

Giving Summary

While God doesn't need your money, He uses your faithful giving to accomplish His purposes here on earth. We are called to be faithful in your giving and trust Him with the results.

Personal Reflection: How much are you giving? How did you choose that amount? When was the last time you increased your giving? Can you trust God to increase your giving now?

Save

"Precious treasure and oil are in a wise man's dwelling, but a foolish man devours it" —Proverbs 21:20.

Goal of Saving: Protect and Provide for Family

For years, we've taught that saving is an essential part of our stewardship responsibility. Within the Five Biblical Financial Priorities, saving comes after giving, and before spending. There are some who have a great issue with this order. Shouldn't we pay our bills before saving? Fortunately, Scripture is not silent on the topic of saving. Based on our study of God's Word, we believe that *the goal of saving is to protect and provide for one's family.* We know that in an ultimate sense, our savings accomplish nothing apart from God's gracious plan. Yet we also know that God often uses things like savings to protect the financial stability of the family when unexpected bills occur. Savings can also prevent the family from going into debt, thus providing a measure of "protection."

God Loves the Family

The priority of saving can first be seen in God's love for family. After He created the world, He created the first family of Adam and Eve. Yet, our first parents disobeyed the Lord, lost fellowship with God, and failed to steward the world. Ever since the Fall, we have all continued to rebel against God. Like the prodigal son who rejected his family, many of us have wandered far from our Heavenly Father, seeking to find joy on our own terms. Yet, unlike the prodigal son, we have an elder brother, Jesus, who came to earth and paid the penalty for our broken relationship with the Father. Through His sacrifice, we are now adopted into God's family. Consider the beauty of **Romans 8:14-16:**

> *"For all who are led by the Spirit of God are sons of God. For you did not receive the spirit of slavery to fall back into fear, but you have received the Spirit of* **adoption as sons**, *by whom we cry,* **'Abba! Father!'** *The Spirit himself bears witness with our spirit that we are* **children of God**.*"* (emphasis added)

How does our adoption into God's family relate to savings?

God loves us so much that he provided all that we need to live for Him in this broken world. Consider **2 Peter 1:3**, which says, "*His divine power has granted to us all things that pertain to life and godliness.*" This verse goes on to explain that the provision is accessed through our knowledge of Him. We echo God's love and care for us when we provide for our family's current and future needs, but human provision is, at best, a dim reflection of God's provision. We are not able to provide for needs to the extent that God can and will, but we are still called to love our families and care for their needs.

When we provide for our families, we don't do so to try to earn God's favor or replace the need for God's provision. We provide because we are following His example, and trusting Him for the results.

1 Timothy 5:8 says, "*But if anyone does not provide for his relatives, and especially for members of his household, he has denied the faith and is worse than an unbeliever.*" In this verse, the word "provide" means more than just a paycheck. It implies that the responsibility to provide is *continuous*. The Good Steward seeks to have a plan for meeting the current and future needs of his family. This requires saving as part of the planning process.

As good stewards, we should set aside part of our income to meet future needs. This means that we should have an emergency fund and retirement savings. We'll discuss these topics in detail later in the book.

Expect the Unexpected

One of the most significant implications of the second law of thermodynamics is that all things tend toward randomness and decay. This is the unfortunate reality of the world we live in, but it wasn't God's original design. God created the world to be perfect and eternal, but when sin entered the world, things began to decay. This means that everything on this earth breaks or eventually wears out. Pastors and theologians often refer to the second law of thermodynamics as "the curse," or "the Fall," and some believers call it "living under the curse."

So, how does the second law of thermodynamics apply to saving money?

You should expect the unexpected. Since everything eventually wears out, the things we own and use will need to be replaced. This means we should expect things to break or wear out and plan accordingly. If you own a home, for instance, we will eventually need to replace the roof. At some point, cars need new tires and require new parts. We can't be surprised when these things happen; we need to be prepared. We need to have a reserve and a plan for replacing these items, otherwise we will go into debt. We'll give guidance and discuss specific strategies for saving in Part Two of the book.

The Necessity of Saving

Many people feel they will save money only if there is money left after paying their bills, but too often they find that there's more month left at the end of their money. Saving must become a conviction, not a convenience. If you feel like you can never get ahead, it's probably because you haven't made saving a priority.

We often teach that *if you don't earn interest, you'll pay interest*. In other words, those who do not have savings will often find that borrowing on credit cards is the only way to handle unexpected bills when emergencies happen. Since they are not earning interest on money that they have in the bank, they are paying interest on money that they've borrowed. I don't know about you, but I'd rather earn interest than pay it. The unfortunate truth is, people often go into debt because they don't save.

But what does the Bible have to say about all of this? Let us consider two verses.

"The prudent sees danger and hides himself, but the simple go on and suffer for it."

Our first verse is repeated twice in the book of **Proverbs** (**22:3** and **27:12**). Whenever a verse is repeated, take note, because it's obviously important. This proverb teaches that both the prudent (another word for "the wise") and the simple (another word for "the fool") look out for potential problems. What separates the wise from the fool is his response. While the fool simply says, "I'll cross that bridge when I get to it," the wise prepares for the potential problem. When it comes to financial stewardship, the Good Steward saves and prepares for future expenses such as, but not limited to, the following: emergencies, college tuition, weddings, car replacements, and retirement. This brings us to the second verse, **Proverbs 21:20**:

"Precious treasure and oil are in a wise man's dwelling, but a foolish man devours it."

In this verse, "precious treasures and oil" are another way of saying "reserves." Notice where the reserves are located. They're not in the house of the rich, rather they are in the house of the *wise*. Having savings and reserves is not necessarily a sign of wealth—it's a sign of wisdom.

You can learn an important lesson from Parkinson's Law, which states: Work expands to fill the time available for its completion. This means your budget will expand to use up all of the income that's available. When you cultivate the habit of giving 10% of your income to church, and saving 10% of your income for future expenses, you will find a way to live off the other 80% of your income.

Some of you may struggle to see how it's possible to save 10% of your income. We realize there are always more buckets to put your money in than money to put in your buckets. However, sacrificing your wants in the moment to make sure the needs of your family are met both today and in the future is of the utmost importance. You save money so you can *have* money.

Spend

"So, whether you eat or drink, or whatever you do, do all to the glory of God" —1 Corinthians 10:31.

So far, we've established that the first financial priority is to honor God through giving, and the second priority is to provide for your family through saving. What comes next? Your third priority is to maintain a godly testimony through being timely and honorable with your creditors. This is commonly referred to as spending.

Our Choices Bring Glory to God

As Christians, we are able to reflect the glory of God to the world through our actions, and God wants us to live a life worthy of our calling. The thematic verse for this section is found in **1 Corinthians 10:31.** Paul wants the church in Corinth to understand that all of their choices matter. **"***So, whether you eat or drink, or whatever you do, do all to the glory of God."* This verse implies that there are essentially two ways to live: We can live by making every choice to please ourselves, or we can choose to honor God in all of our choices. Even small choices can bring glory to God, and this is true when it comes to how we choose to spend our money. Let's consider three additional verses as they relate to our financial choices:

1. Paying Taxes - *"Pay to all what is owed to them: taxes to whom taxes are owed, revenue to whom revenue is owed"* (**Romans 13:7**).
2. Paying Debts - *"The wicked borrows but does not pay back"* (**Psalm 37:21**).
3. Financial Independence - *"Aspire to live quietly, and to mind your own affairs, and to work with your hands, as we instructed you, so that you may walk properly before outsiders and be dependent on no one"* (**1 Thessalonians 4:11–12**).

Prioritization

As we stated previously, the way you handle your money reveals your true priorities. Your spending habits reveal what you love and value most. Have you ever thought about what your spending says about you? If someone reviewed your bank account or credit card statements, what would they say is most important in your life?

We realize that spending money is inevitable, but applying the Five Biblical Financial Priorities can help you make the right choices. You need to pay the mortgage or rent, put food on the table, and keep the lights on. Spending money on essentials for living is called "necessity spending." However, not all spending decisions are equal, and you need to prioritize your spending between needs and wants.

Overspending

When you don't prioritize, this can lead to overspending, which is easy to do if you aren't careful. In fact, many of us *don't even know* we do it. Read the following examples and see if you have any of these overspending habits.

Trips to Big Box Stores: How many times do you walk into one of the many big box stores with the intent of buying a few specific items, only to leave the store with several unnecessary purchases?

Coffee/Convenience Stores: What's a few bucks to grab a coffee, latte, or a snack on the way to work? How much do you spend on convenience store sandwiches each week? Gourmet coffee drinks are expensive, and convenience stores significantly mark up their items. The cost of these stops adds up quickly.

Subscriptions: Those cheap and infrequently used movie and music subscriptions or gym memberships may be punching a bigger hole in your bank account than you think.

Eating Out: You all have busy lives, and the convenience of eating out can be a lifesaver at times. You should plan ahead to limit eating out unnecessarily. For example, you can pack a lunch and take it to work. There's nothing wrong with going out to eat, but it should be considered a luxury, not a necessity.

Frequent Use of Credit Cards: As referenced below, we tend to spend more with credit cards than when we pay in cash.

Spend on Purpose… use a Budget

Many studies show that spending with a credit card is psychologically different than using cash. This leads to overspending when you pay with a credit card. This is in part why the average American family has between $5,000 and $10,000 in credit card debt[3]. For some reason, many people think that the word "budget" is an expletive, never to be used or uttered in their home. They view budgets as restrictive and hard to follow. Yes, there are often several factors which make budgeting difficult at first, but persisting through them is worth it. Just like anything good in life, the reward for perseverance far outweighs the initial inconvenience.

It can also be helpful to think of a budget as a road map to reach your destination. You wouldn't dream of driving to a place you've never been before without using a map app on your phone, right? By creating a spending plan (or budget), you can give marching orders to your money by prioritizing what you do with your hard-earned income.

Living within our means gets easier with time—the key is to develop good personal-spending habits, and to recognize when it's necessary to review and alter our budget. You can find a copy of our budget worksheets in the resource section of our website (www.thelifegroup.org).

If you are struggling to make a budget work, we have found the following tips to be helpful.

1. **Groceries:**
   a. Make a meal plan for the week and shop to fill a menu, rather than fill the pantry. When you shop to fill the pantry, you inevitably purchase and consume more food than you would have otherwise.
   b. Consider shopping at discount food or "dent and ding" stores. Oftentimes, you can get great deals on food. Just be sure to check the expiration date before purchasing.
2. **Insurance:**
   a. Shop for home and auto insurance coverage every four to five years. The longer you are with a carrier, the more likely you can find a cheaper policy elsewhere.

---

[3] In our research, there was no consistant number for how much debt individuals or families caried but they were almost all between $5k and $10k.

    b. Try to pay your insurance premiums annually. Most insurers offer a discount for premiums paid all at once, rather than in monthly installments.

3. **Save Now, Buy Later:**
   a. Avoid impulse purchases and the "buy now, pay later" craze. If you wait before purchasing an item, you may find that you don't need it after all.

4. **Personal Allowance:**
   a. You can limit excess personal spending by creating a monthly budget with a fixed dollar amount. This allows you to occasionally grab a coffee on the go, but within the parameters of your intentional discretionary budgeted dollars.

Offerings

"Religion that is pure and undefiled before God the Father is this: to visit orphans and widows in their affliction, and to keep oneself unstained from the world" —James 1:27.

Well, you've given to your local church, saved for retirement, spent money on the necessities of life, and now you get to spend on yourselves, right? Not quite yet. Your fourth financial priority is Offerings. Offerings? Isn't that just another word for tithes or giving? No, it isn't. The Five Biblical Financial Priorities clearly distinguish between giving (or tithing) and offerings.

Giving contributes to the local church and its general fund. *Offerings* are giving above and beyond the tithe. This includes giving to special funds for the church (building fund, missions fund, deacons fund), giving to parachurch or nonprofit organizations, and finally, giving direct cash or non-cash assistance to the poor and needy.

Exodus 35-36 gives us a beautiful example of offerings. Moses, speaking for God, asks the people of Israel, for a "*contribution to the LORD*" – a "freewill offering" – saying, "*Whoever is of a generous heart, let him bring the LORD's contribution*" (**Exodus 35:5b**). Moses then goes on to list all of the specific materials needed for building the tabernacle according to God's directions. As we read the remainder of chapter 35 and into 36, we read repeated phrases like *"everyone whose heart stirred him," "everyone whose spirit moved him," "all who were of a willing heart," "all the women whose hearts stirred them,"* and *"all the men and women, whose heart moved them"* describing the freewill offerings given every morning. Finally, the two craftsmen in charge of building the tabernacle came to Moses telling him that the people brought *"much more than enough for doing the work that the LORD has commanded us to do. So Moses gave command…, "Let no man or woman do anything more for the contribution for the sanctuary"* (**Exodus 36:5-6a**). The narration then continues: *"So the people were restrained from bringing, for the material they had was sufficient to do all the work, and more"* (**Exodus 36:6b-7**). We would do well to have such generous, willing hearts to give to the specific funds or needs of the local church beyond the general fund.

There are many great ministries that support the work of the church and that meet the spiritual and physical needs of those in the community and around the world. Offerings is where you get to allocate a portion of your budget to support this important work. While it may be appropriate for the lion's share of your giving to go toward Christian organizations, it may also be appropriate to support certain secular non-profits that are doing good in this world. Let's look at what the Bible says about your responsibilities to the less fortunate.

- *"If a man shuts his ears to the cry of the poor, he too will cry out and not be answered"* (**Proverbs 21:13**).
- *"He who gives to the poor will never want, But he who shuts his eyes will have many curses"* (**Proverbs 28:27**).
- *"Let the thief no longer steal, but rather let him labor, doing honest work with his own hands, so that he may have something to share with anyone in need"* (**Ephesians 4:28**).
- *"Religion that is pure and undefiled before God the Father is this: to visit orphans and widows in their affliction, and to keep oneself unstained from the world"* (**James 1:27**).

The Third Tithe
Earlier, we discussed that the Old Testament describes three different tithes: 10% for the Levites, 10% for the festivals, and 10% for

the poor. It is upon this third tithe that we base much of our thinking regarding offerings. **Deuteronomy 14** outlines God's expectations for how His children should care for the less fortunate:

> *"At the end of every three years you shall bring out all the tithe of your produce in the same year and lay it up within your towns. And the Levite, because he has no portion or inheritance with you, and the sojourner, the fatherless, and the widow, who are within your towns, shall come and eat and be filled, that the LORD your God may bless you in all the work of your hands that you do"* (**Deuteronomy 14:28–29**)..

God cares about the plight of the poor. Note the different classes of individuals that are highlighted in this passage. First, the Levites are included as recipients of this offering because the nature of their calling limited their ability to provide for their own needs. They served God by serving the nation, and in their doing so, the nation was to assist in meeting their needs. This is similar to the situation of those called to full-time vocational ministry. Not only pastors (**1 Timothy 5:17**), but missionaries, teachers, camp workers, and other ministry support personnel serve the body of Christ and as such should be supported by the body that they serve (**1 Timothy 6:17-19**). Many ministries do not pay a living wage to those called to do the work. As believers, we need to make sure that the individuals who are faithfully serving are fairly compensated for their labor.

Second, sojourners, strangers, and foreigners matter to God. As a church, we should have an open and hospitable attitude toward those who are far from their native bases of support. There are two great Biblical reasons for caring for strangers:

1. God's people are filled with compassion for wanderers as they remember the wilderness wandering of their forefathers.
2. As Christians, we too are wanderers and strangers in this world. Consider **Matthew 25:35**, *"I was a stranger and you welcomed me."* We'll discuss these points in more detail in the next section.

Finally, the fatherless and widows are dearly loved by God. We treat these two as one group because they are created by the loss of the same person. When a woman loses her husband, or a child his father, great suffering—not just emotional, but also financial—occurs.

God doesn't just understand the plight of the fatherless and widow intellectually. Jesus lost His earthly father. His mother was widowed. He has experienced this loss and pain. This is why, in part, Jesus charged John to care for Mary as He was dying on the cross (**John 19:26-27**).

So, whose responsibility is it to care for widows? God through Paul commanded that children should be the first to provide for their widowed mothers (**1 Timothy 5:3-8**). However, if a widow is truly alone and without support, it is then the role of the church to provide for her needs (**1 Timothy 5:9-10**).

The Least of These

As Jesus' ministry and life moved closer to the grand climax of His death and resurrection, He took His disciples up to the Mount of Olives, which overlooked Jerusalem, and taught them about many things that were about to happen. Some of those things would usher in the end of the world. Late in this discourse, He describes the final judgment of man. This passage, found in **Matthew 25:31–46**, is worth careful consideration:

> *34) Then the King will say to those on his right, 'Come, you who are blessed by my Father, inherit the kingdom prepared for you from the foundation of the world. 35) For I was hungry and you gave me food, I was thirsty and you gave me drink, I was a stranger and you welcomed me, 36) I was naked and you clothed me, I was sick and you visited me, I was in prison and you came to me.' 37) Then the righteous will answer him, saying, 'Lord, when did we see you hungry and feed you, or thirsty and give you drink? 38) And when did we see you a stranger and welcome you, or naked and clothe you? 39) And when did we see you sick or in prison and visit you?' 40) And the King will answer them, 'Truly, I say to you, as you did it to one of the least of these my brothers, you did it to me.'* (**vs 34-40**).

Offerings are such an important part of the Good Steward's financial life because when you serve the less fortunate in Christ's name, you are serving God. It's as if the acts of kindness and mercy were done to God Himself. We urge you, for the sake of your eternal joy and happiness, to seek to meet the needs of others around you. Moving toward your fellow man moves you closer to the heart of God!

While you're called to give to the poor, you must do so with wisdom and discernment, and trust God to lead you in your best judgment. One book that may be helpful as you consider the best way to provide assistance to the poor is *When Helping Hurts: How to Alleviate Poverty Without Hurting the Poor . . . and Yourself©,* by Steve Corbett and Brian Fikkert (2014, Moody Publishers).

Purpose of Prosperity

In his book *The Treasure Principle©*, author Randy Alcorn says, "God prospers us not to raise our standard of living, but to raise our standard of giving[3]." We wholeheartedly agree with this statement. Our hearts should be filled with the compassion of Christ to help those in need. Owning possessions is not in and of itself sinful, but when the pursuit of more and more means that we give less and less, we are missing the point of God's blessing.

God blesses us so that we will be a blessing to others. Consider what God told Abraham when He established the covenant with him, *"I will surely bless you, and I will surely multiply your offspring… and **in your offspring shall all the nations of the earth be blessed**, because you have obeyed my voice"* (**Genesis 22:17–18**, emphasis added). While this promise is fulfilled in the person and work of Jesus Christ, we also see its fulfillment, albeit to a lesser extent, when we use our blessings to bless others.

Therefore, part of the Christian call is to open your eyes and ears to the cries of the poor and answer them. An offering can be as formal as supporting a particular mission or non-profit organization, or as informal as buying groceries for a neighbor who lost his job and needs to support three kids. You could also choose to support a fund outside of your local church's general fund, such as the building fund. If finances are tight, offerings can also be giving your time and resources rather than money.

Luxuries

"...God richly provides us with everything to enjoy" —1 Timothy 6:17.

God is the giver of all good things–including luxuries. This means that luxuries aren't a bad thing, but they shouldn't be our top priority.

So, what is a luxury?

According to the *Merriam-Webster Dictionary*, luxury is defined as "a) something adding to pleasure or comfort but not absolutely necessary; b) an indulgence in something that provides pleasure, satisfaction, or ease." A luxury is not truly essential to your survival—the main idea is that a luxury is a "nice to have," not a "need to have."

What do Luxuries Look Like?

God is not obligated to provide material blessings to His children, though often He does. At this point, it will be helpful to remember where luxuries fit into the Five Biblical Financial Priorities. Keep in mind, luxuries are not your first priority, they are your fifth priority.

- First, if you are not giving to the Lord, you have no room for luxuries.
- Second, if you are not saving for your family, you have no room for luxuries.
- Third, if you are not spending (meeting your financial obligations), you have no room for luxuries.
- Fourth, if you are not budgeting for offerings, you have no room for luxuries.

It's important for you to identify the expenses in your lives that are luxuries. When finances are tight, you shouldn't be going out to eat. You shouldn't spend money on cable TV or streaming services or binge shop online. You may need to steer clear of subscription services while you save. These things are all nice to have, but they aren't essential for your survival. You can't manage your finances and become good stewards if you prioritize having cable over paying your mortgage.

The Most Important Question about Luxuries

Should luxuries even be a priority? Should you just meet your needs then give the rest of your money away? With all of the struggles, and all of the unevangelized people of this world, why should you enjoy luxuries at all? These are important questions. However, the most important question, in our opinion, is does God care about your joy?

The Westminster Shorter Catechism Question #1 asks, "What is the chief end [goal or purpose] of man?" The Answer says, "The chief end of man is to glorify God and enjoy Him forever." Notice that one of the reasons God has created us is to find our joy in Him. God cares deeply for His glory and our joy. Consider the following verses:

- *"These things I have spoken to you, that my joy may be in you, and that* **your joy may be full"** (**John 15:11**, emphasis added).
- *"But the fruit of the Spirit is love,* **joy,** *peace…"* (**Galatians 5:22**, emphasis added).
- *"…in your presence there is* **fullness of joy;** *at your right hand are* **pleasures forevermore"** (**Psalm 16:11**, emphasis added).

What does all of this have to do with luxuries? A joyless life does not bring glory to God. He blesses us with many things (both material and immaterial) to bring us joy and show His favor to us. While you can still have a joyful life without luxuries, God blesses us with many things. If God provides material wealth, it is not wrong to enjoy it within the framework of the Five Biblical Financial Priorities. It's not wrong to live in a nice house, drive a nice car, and have nice things, provided that these things don't become all-consuming.

Another major consideration regarding luxuries is how much is enough and how much is too much? We can't answer that question for you. That is between you and the Lord. However, we do want you to consider intentionally spending less on luxuries so that you can allocate more for Kingdom purposes (i.e., supporting ministry and mission efforts).

Let's return to the questions we asked at the beginning of this section: What about giving to missions? What about helping the poor? Our answer is that if you are living according to the financial framework that we've shared, you have already been giving to your local church and looking for ways to support and bless those who are less fortunate through offerings. If this is true, then enjoying luxuries is acceptable, but we do have a word of caution about conspicuous consumerism. In this next section, we'll examine several dangers of luxuries.

The Danger of Luxuries

"Adversity hath slain her thousands, but prosperity her ten thousands." —Thomas Brooks

We can overemphasize any one of the Five Biblical Financial Priorities, leading to an unhealthy relationship with money. For example, we can put such an emphasis on Priority 1: Giving, that we expect God to materially bless us, or we think God is in debt to us. We can focus so much on Priority 2: Savings, that our trust shifts to our savings, rather than to God, who promises to provide. We can also overemphasize Priority 5: Luxuries, which can harm the heart of the steward and be a danger to our souls.

Danger 1: Luxuries Become a Right

Those who have put into practice the first four financial priorities could think that the payoff for all of their hard work thus far is finally here. Now, they can enjoy themselves and their abundance. They think that luxuries are their right or reward for giving, saving, paying bills on time, and giving to others. The truth is that luxuries are a gift from God; they are not fares for good behavior. Don't allow yourself to believe that God owes you abundance and ease in this life. They may come in this life, but if not, for those who trust Him here and now, they will absolutely come in eternity.

Danger 2: Unhealthy Fixation on this World

Jesus commanded His listeners not to store up treasures on earth (**Matthew 6:19**). In **Luke 12**, we learn of the rich fool who tore down his barns to build bigger barns. Jesus starts the story with this warning, *"Take care, and be on your guard against all covetousness, for one's life does not consist in the abundance of his possessions"* (**Luke 12:15**). When the rich fool thought about his abundance, he concluded that he should maximize his joy in this life, saying, *"relax, eat, drink, be merry…"* (**vs 19**). It is right to enjoy God's blessings as an act of worship to Him, the Giver of all good things. It is wrong to enjoy abundance without acknowledging our good and gracious God who provided the blessing.

It is a great loss to only focus on maximizing joy here and now, without any thought of securing great joy for all eternity. Hear Christ's words to you: *"But lay up for yourselves treasures in heaven… for where your treasure is, there your heart will be also"* (**Matthew 6:20-21**).

Danger 3: We Become Discontent

Contentment is difficult. We often think that if we only had a little more, then we would be happy, but really, the more we have, the more we want. Paul warns those who are rich to not put their confidence in *"the uncertainty of riches"* (**1 Timothy 6:17**). Rather, they are to trust in God. No amount of possessions or money can provide true contentment. The author of the book of Hebrews states, *"Keep your life free from love of money, and be content with what you have, for he has said, 'I will never leave you nor forsake you'"* (**Hebrews 13:5**). The basis for your contentment is not the amount of stuff you have, the size of your investment portfolios, or your income. Your contentment is founded upon the infallible promise of God to "never leave us nor forsake us." Luxuries can't match that promise.

Danger 4: Exploit the Poor to Acquire More

There are many texts in Scripture that address the rich abusing the poor. For example, consider **James 5:1–5**: *"Come now, you rich, weep and howl for the miseries that are coming upon you… Behold, **the wages of the laborers** who mowed your fields, which **you kept back by fraud**, are crying out against you… You have lived on the earth in luxury and in self-indulgence. You have fattened your hearts in a day of slaughter"* (emphasis added). While today's workers have greater legal protections than the workers that James speaks of, we still have employers using manipulative practices to avoid paying employees what is their right under the law. Rather than treating wage earners as a resource to be used, employers should seek to invest into their teams in a way that honors the workers' dignity and worth, while being mindful of the bottom line. We are convinced that a motivated and fairly compensated workforce will create value for customers and owners alike. .

Danger 5: Excessive Luxuries Can Cause Spiritual Harm

Let us simply point out the various harms that the love and pursuit of money can bring. In **1 Timothy 6:9-10,** Paul says that those who make the pursuit of wealth their chief goal 1) enter into temptation, 2) are caught in a trap, 3) bring ruin and destruction, and 4) pierce themselves with many pangs. In this passage, Paul also makes the profound statement that *"the love of money is the root of all kinds of evil."* We'll discuss 1 Timothy 6 in greater detail later in the book.

In **Mark 4:19,** Jesus says that *"the cares of this world and the deceitfulness of riches and the desires for other things enter in and choke the word."* When gaining possessions becomes your passion and goal, there is no room left for the Word of God to take root in your heart.

Danger 6: Luxuries Feed Pride, Selfishness, and Self-Confidence

Paul addresses the rich in **1 Timothy 6:17,** charging them not to be haughty. Other translations use the terms "arrogant," "proud," and "conceited". Wealth has a particular way of overinflating our sense of worth, while demeaning the worth of those who have less.

Consider the message of **Jeremiah 9:23–24:** *"Thus says the LORD: '...let not the rich man boast in his riches, but let him who boasts boast in this, that he understands and knows me, that I am the LORD who practices steadfast love, justice, and righteousness in the earth. For in these things I delight, declares the LORD.'"* The size of our savings account does not impress God. Frankly, it's only God's opinion of us that ultimately matters. Rather than making wealth your chief pursuit, seek to know God and live in a way that brings Him honor and glory. That's something worth getting excited over.

Worship: The Proper use of Luxuries

We understand that having luxuries is not necessarily wrong, but they carry with them special dangers. So what is the proper way to use or enjoy luxuries?

Luxuries are rightly to be enjoyed as a celebration of all that God has done for you. Not only has He saved you, redeemed you, and provided for your needs, but He also has given you many of your wants. God gives you more than you could ever ask, think of, or imagine, and luxuries are a great blessing from Him. God delights in your enjoyment of Him and all that He has given and provided, so when you enjoy luxuries the right way, essentially, you are worshiping God.

Remember what we said in Chapter One. We are all worshipers. If we are not worshiping God, then we are worshiping something He has created. Luxuries can easily replace God as the central focus of our joy. However, when enjoyed with a heart toward God, luxuries point us to the Giver of the good gifts who deserves all of our worship and praise.

Shame Culture

Unfortunately, we live in a society that shames people in the church who have money. To give an example, in his book, *The Legacy Journey: A Radical View of Biblical Wealth and Generosity*, Dave Ramsey (2014, Ramsey Press) talks about a billionaire who drove an expensive luxury car. Ramsey had dinner with him, and afterward, this rich man apologized for owning the vehicle. He said he knew he could have been a better steward, and applied the money elsewhere. He knew people were looking down on him in judgment. Ramsey looked at him and said the man had made large, notable, charitable donations in the previous year, compared to the cost of his car. There was nothing wrong with this man driving a luxury car, because he was living out the Biblical call to bless others.

The point is, we are not to pass judgment on others if they are wealthy, and we can't make assumptions about how they spend their money. We have no idea how truly generous they might be.

On the other hand, if we're rich, we are not to shame or judge the poor. We can't assume they've mismanaged their money, or they don't know how to save. We don't know the details of their situation.

But whether rich or poor, we've been called to steward *our own assets*. We aren't called to steward the assets of others. God provides all things, and He trusts us to manage our money and care for our possessions according to His Word.

What to Do with Surplus Income?

As the size of one's income increases, their lifestyle tends to increase as well. The more one earns. the more one spends. Is this the right way to handle a growing income? We recommend that as income increases beyond what is needed to meet one's basic needs, an increase in the amount of giving (both to church and to others) is in order. While it may not be necessary to give all your surplus away, it would be good to ask God how much of this increase to keep for yourself. Remember, if God has blessed you with financial wealth, it's not for your own gain; it's so you can be a greater blessing to others.

Treasures in Heaven

"Do not lay up for yourselves treasures on earth, where moth and rust destroy and where thieves break in and steal, but lay up for yourselves treasures in heaven, where neither moth nor rust destroy, and where thieves do not break in and steal. For where your treasure is, there your heart will be also"—Matthew 6:19-21.

We understand that taking steps toward becoming a good steward can be a battle. The world has conditioned us to think that luxuries come before necessities. We think that earthly treasures are most valuable, and it can be difficult to break free from that mindset. The previous verse from Matthew says you are not to invest your wealth and resources in earthly things, but you are to trust in the Lord and send it ahead. You can store your treasures in heaven, but this doesn't mean a literal treasure waits for you there. It means that generosity in this life has eternal rewards, and you may experience greater joy, honor, and delight in heaven.

There's nothing wrong with having and enjoying luxuries, but you need to make sure you don't *worship* them. Luxuries come from God, and He is the One you should truly worship. You should rightly and properly enjoy luxuries because they are given by God, the Giver of all good things.

Conclusion: Biblical Priorities vs. Worldly Priorities

Throughout this chapter, you've considered the Five Biblical Financial Priorities, and now you know them in your head. It can often be difficult, however, to live them out in your decisions and actions, and this is where understanding the influence of the world around you can help.

As Biblical stewards, you are called to give, save, spend, make offerings, and then spend on luxuries. But the world says that *you* are the most important person, and *you* should take care of yourself first, because no one else will take care of you. The world spends on luxuries first, pays bills second, and if there's money left over at the end of the month, you could save it. It's rare for the world to give—giving tends to be an afterthought.

THE WORLD	BE TRANSFORMED	BIBLICAL STEWARDSHIP
1. Luxuries		1. Give
2. Offerings		2. Save
3. Spend		3. Spend
4. Save		4. Offerings
5. Give	ROMANS 12:2	5. Luxuries

Instead of falling under the influence of the world's view of money, the Biblical steward should embrace the instruction given in **Romans 12:2**: *"Do not be conformed to this world, but be transformed by the renewal of your mind."* As you allow the Word of God to shape your thoughts on how to prioritize your finances, you will find that your actions follow suit. As demonstrated above, the Good Steward has a radically different ordering of his priorities than that of the rest of the world.

PART 2 - The Good Steward's Call

Chapter 4:

Training the Next Generation

Now that we have an understanding of the Five Biblical Financial Priorities, let's discuss the responsibility that we have as parents to train the next generation. At this point, some readers may choose to skip this chapter because they have no children, or their children are grown and out of the house. While this temptation is understandable, there still is great value here, even for those who are not raising children, because our emphasis on the heart applies to every human regardless of age.

A special note for grandparents: You have a very special and powerful role to play in the training of your children and grandchildren. As outside observers, you may have the perspective to gently encourage your children in their parenting roles. By sharing your life and potentially even your resources with your grandchildren, you can help them develop into good stewards.

For childless individuals: In the church, we all play an important role in helping each other rear our children in the nurture and admonition of the Lord. You have more influence than you may think! Even if you do not have children, you should strive to use your time, talents, and treasures to aid in the spiritual and stewardship formation of the next generation. We hope that the ideas in this chapter will be encouraging to you even if you have to adapt how you apply them.

Shepherding the Heart and Wallet

"Train up a child in the way he should go; even when he is old he will not depart from it" —Proverbs 22:6.

The greatest role of Christian parents is to train their children to follow Christ. We believe that parents are called to do three things when it comes to children and stewardship. First and foremost, parents are to help their children see the surpassing worth and value of a life devoted to serving God with all they have, and to show their children that God matters more than money. Second, parents are called to model good stewardship to their children. The values and priorities that parents demonstrate will greatly influence the values and priorities of their children. Finally, parents are to talk with their children about the dangers of loving money and possessions above God.

Our words and actions as parents have a profound influence on our children. Think about how you respond to your child when he or she demands or requests something. If you are like most parents, you'll probably respond in one of two ways: The first response might be something like, "Do you think money grows on trees? Do you have any idea how hard I work just to get ahead? I'm not going to spend my money on that!" This response can shame your children. It also teaches them that a lack of money is the problem, therefore more money will solve all life's problems. Our children might begin equating happiness with money, leading them down a dangerous road.

The second way you might respond is with indulgence. You don't want to say no to your children, so you may be tempted to throw money at your kids. Sadly, giving in to the demands of your children is easier than having important conversations about money and priorities. This practice deprives children of understanding the relationship between work and earning money. It also reinforces their natural inclination to give in to every desire, and they don't learn the value of delayed gratification.

To ensure that your children properly value money, avoid the cycle of debt, and don't fall under the influence of the world, parents should teach and demonstrate several important stewardship lessons. First, and most importantly, your children must learn that because God made all that exists, He owns everything. This is made clear in passages like **Deuteronomy 10:14,** *"Behold, to the Lord your God belong heaven and the heaven of heavens, the earth with all that is in it."* Second, they need to learn that they are caretakers of all that God provides to them. Finally, as stewards, your children need to handle what God has entrusted to them in the way He requires. They can't mistreat or misuse the resources entrusted to them by God. Understanding these three truths will affect the way that children handle money. They'll begin to see that the purpose of money is to serve God and others.

To prepare your children for a life of Biblical stewardship, you should talk with them about finances early and often. It would be wonderful if every family with young children started out this way, but not all of them do. Sadly, many parents expect their children will learn about finances and debt in school or college. Not only do most schools not offer this training, but the limited schools that do offer such programs do not teach Biblical stewardship. There should be no substitute for family-based training so that your children can become good stewards. If you haven't been talking with your children about stewardship, you can start now. You haven't failed, and it's not too late.

You may feel that talking to your kids about money is hypocritical, especially if you're new to financial stewardship yourself. You may think, *Who am I to try and teach my children about something I don't know well?* This is a common feeling for many parents. The truth is, your kids don't expect you to be perfect—they expect honesty and some level of transparency. Simply let them know you're starting to learn about stewardship yourself, and you want them to join you on this journey as you work to get on the right path.

If your children begin to learn with you now, regardless of their age, they'll have a greater chance of avoiding mistakes in the future, and will experience greater success. With your help and guidance, they'll learn how to properly plan, budget, save, and spend.

Not A Guarantee

As mentioned in Chapter 1, Proverbs are general observations about how the world works. They reflect the normal relationship between an action or idea and its result. We must be careful not to turn proverbs into some kind of promise, such as, if you do A, the result will always and in every instance be B.

The well-known **Proverb, 22:6** says, *"Train up a child in the way he should go; even when he is old he will not depart from it."* It's important to note that because this is a proverb, it's not a promise. We can't promise or guarantee that your kids will make all the right choices as a result of your stewardship training. As parents, we're called to do all we can to help shape our children's mindsets and values, but there's no way for us to control what they do. However, teaching them Biblical stewardship gives them the best chance of properly managing their finances in adulthood.

If You Don't Teach Them, Someone Else Will

Children are sponges. They are always learning from everything they see, and everyone they meet. This means the habits and behaviors parents demonstrate have a great impact on their worldview. In fact, a Barna Research Group study on "Children Developing Their Worldview[4]" (2003) discovered the following:

› By age two, a child's worldview is already starting to develop.

› By age nine, a child's moral foundation is generally in place.

› By age thirteen, a child's worldview is practically set in stone.

These results indicate the importance of being proactive as a parent and teaching our children the Biblical view of money early in their lives. We need to have regular conversations with them that increase in depth and complexity as they get older, and do the same when entrusting them with financial responsibilities. While these results show the importance of starting early, it's never too late to teach your children

---

[4] https://www.barna.com/research/a-biblical-worldview-has-a-radical-effect-on-a-persons-life/.

or teens new concepts. Even as adults, we are still learning and reshaping our thoughts and habits.

Even when our children go to college or move out, our job as parents doesn't end. They will still need guidance and encouragement from us. Having stewardship conversations with them early and often sets the precedent that we are a trusted source who can provide godly advice about finances, even when they're adults. They can still turn to us when they have questions or need help.

Money's Influence on Marriage

Stewardship education (or lack thereof) can influence the future of your children in various ways, and not all of them are financial. As we've talked with pastors and counselors across the country, we've found that financial issues and mismanagement of money are a leading cause of marital conflict. It's commonly cited that nearly half of marriages end in divorce. It is our prayer that children who are raised in homes where Biblical financial stewardship is taught and modeled will be less likely to experience marital stress and potential divorce.

In our experience, the core issue in most marriages isn't the money per se, but the way materialism or consumerism influences spending priorities. Materialism is the belief that happiness is directly related to the amount of one's material possessions. Consumerism is the belief that the very act of purchasing goods and services is what brings happiness. These beliefs are clearly unbiblical, but can subtly seep into marriages and cause serious damage. The desire for more can lead to spending more than one should to have the appearance of affluence or success. This overspending leaves a couple weighed down with debt which, over time, leaves them unable to get ahead financially, or even break even. They are always putting out financial fires by robbing Peter to pay Paul. This creates intense stress and conflict in the marriage, as there is no room for them to spend as they would like. This is because their credit is tapped out, and/or their minimum payments become more than they can handle.

These consequences lead them to ask if they are teaching their children to be content with what they have? Are they modeling contentment in their financial choices?

Another question to consider is, have you taught your child to value God more than money? What will happen in your children's marriages if God sees fit to bless them with abundance? One study shows that 70 percent of men who make six times more than minimum wage admit to some type of infidelity. The wrong attitude or mindset about wealth can lead to self-indulgence, not just with finances, but with sex, also. When we earn more income than those around us, we can become conceited and self-focused. Rather than seeing money as a means to worship God and serve others, those with abundance might view money as a means to gratify themselves. Does your child have a craving for wealth and abundance without the moral character to handle it wisely?

In his book *Precious Remedies Against Satan's Devices*, Puritan author Thomas Brooks says, "Adversity hath slain her thousands but prosperity her ten thousands[5]." This is a sobering thought. We spend much time equipping our children to deal with hard circumstances in life, but how much time do we spend preparing them to maintain their trust in God and their dependence on Him when things are going well?

As parents or grandparents, you can help your children form a God-honoring view of money and become good stewards. You have a great opportunity to help your children value their relationship with God and their spouse, whether they have a little money, or a lot.

Instructing Your Children

"And these words... shall be on your heart. You shall teach them diligently to your children, and shall talk of them when you sit in your house, and when you walk by the way, and when you lie down, and when you rise"—Deuteronomy 6:6-7.

This passage clearly emphasizes that parents have a critical role in the lives of their children. It's their job to instruct them in the ways of

---

[5] Banner of Truth, 2011, Page 30

the Lord, and to set a godly example of a Christian life. Many families find it difficult to make time for family worship or devotions. Your kids' schedules are so packed with activities that priorities of eternal significance get displaced. While stewardship is not the most important lesson to teach your children, it is important, and is too often neglected.

The book of Deuteronomy paints a clear picture of the parent/child relationship. It says that parents are to be intentional, proactive, and consistent in teaching their children. The Lord understands that children learn in a variety of ways. They learn from what they hear (teaching), what they see (modeling), and what they do (engaging).

The word "diligently" in verse 7 indicates that there should be intentionality and repetition in your efforts. Having a single conversation or leading by example once a month isn't enough to build a solid foundation or understanding of Biblical stewardship. You need to understand that training your children in Biblical stewardship is a life-long process, not an event. Your children will not develop the essential habits and skills of stewardship after just a few conversations. Since stewardship is a lifestyle, this teaching should be consistent, and you'll need to demonstrate how to be good stewards of your finances and resources.

Christian parents should have a plan to teach, model, and engage their children in the Christian life. With regard to stewardship, you should have a plan for how you'll convey the lifestyle of biblical stewardship to your children. In the next section of this chapter, we will share two ideas that parents can use to teach and engage your children with aspects of financial stewardship.

Don't Go It Alone

Ideally, married couples should approach family stewardship together and hold each other accountable in leading their children. However, sometimes one spouse may not be completely on board, or the busyness of life makes consistent implementation a struggle. It may also be difficult to be consistent if you are a grandparent or single parent. When this is the case, having an outside accountability partner can be beneficial, because an accountability partner can help you remain steadfast in teaching your children Biblical stewardship.

If your spouse is unable to be your accountability partner, it can be a friend from church, a friend from work, another believer, or someone you know to be a good steward. This person can continually remind you of your goals, and encourage you to stay consistent. Your accountability partner can keep you on track, and help you model wise stewardship to your children.

Stewardship Training Ideas

In the remaining sections of this chapter, we'll give specific examples of how we've talked with our children, helped them practice Biblical stewardship through hands-on teaching methods, and invited them into the joys of stewardship and giving as a family.

Handling Money

A simple way to begin teaching your children Biblical stewardship is to give them money of their own so they can learn how to handle it. This is probably the most effective way to facilitate conversations about financial management. It is well understood that children (and adults) learn better through hands-on experience, rather than lectures and other formal training.

The money parents give to children is often referred to as an "allowance." Experts have differing opinions about whether an allowance should be a sharing of household income, or pay for work rendered, such as chores. Each method has its pros and cons, and parents should explore what will work best for them and their families.

For the sake of this book, we prefer that allowance not be payment for work rendered. When dealing with young children between the ages of four and twelve, payment for chores could unintentionally convert a family relationship into a purely economic transaction. In our view, children should do chores because they are members of the household. If a child chooses to not complete their chores because they don't feel that money is enough of an incentive, they aren't grasping the purpose of chores. Without the allowance (or chore money) they will miss out on the opportunity of learning how to properly handle it. Children should do chores as a contribution to the family, not as a monetary transaction.

When introducing the concept of allowance to your children, start by talking about the fact that God provides your income, and you want to share that income with them. You want them to learn how to handle the money that God has entrusted to you. Giving your children an allowance isn't just a practical way to help them learn how to manage finances; it's also a way for them to make mistakes in the safety of your home. If they mess up, at least they're under your supervision at home, and they can learn from their experiences.

Four Quarter Method (Elementary Age Children, K-5)

When my siblings and I (Tim) were young, our mom and dad sat with us on Sunday mornings and gave each of us four quarters. We used separate piggy banks and other storage containers to separate the quarters into the following four categories:

- **1st Quarter for God**—We gave to God first. We were instructed to take this quarter with us to church and place it in the offering.
- **2nd Quarter for Short-term savings**—We learned that we would need to save money for birthdays, Christmas, and vacations.
- **3rd Quarter for Long-term savings**—Even though we didn't fully understand why, our parents explained that we needed to save money for future expenses such as college tuition, or to buy a car or house when we grew up..
- **4th Quarter for ourselves**—My dad called the fourth quarter "discretionary." He said we could do whatever we

wanted with the last quarter. We could save it, spend it, or give it away.

Because we were all young, our parents gave us our allowance weekly. This repetition helped us to learn the basics of giving, saving, and spending, which laid the foundation for learning and applying the Five Biblical Financial Priorities when we were a bit older. Giving us our allowance on Sunday mornings also helped us follow through on our commitment to give a quarter to church each week. We didn't have time to imagine how we could spend God's quarter on ourselves. Needless to say, we all looked forward to Sunday mornings!

The Christmas Match

Around Christmas time, a major event occurred in our household that centered around the four quarter method. We emptied our long-term savings, and if the amount matched or exceeded the minimum amount expected, our parents would double the entire amount saved, and put the money into a mutual fund for our college savings. There would be no match if it was less than what was expected, but the funds were collected and invested, nonetheless. My dad said that he wanted to bless wisdom, not foolishness. The savings match was his way of blessing wise behaviors.

Principles and Guidelines

In addition, the four quarter method has the following principles and guidelines:

- This system teaches giving, rather than tithing. Young children need to learn ownership (it's all God's money) and priorities (giving before spending). Tithing is a concept taught to children with the Envelope System, which we'll explain in the next section.
- Use three different piggy banks or jars for each category. (A giving jar is generally not needed, as children usually give that money right away).
- Always have a reserve. Never spend all of the money.
- Live within your means. This means:
  - No borrowing from siblings

- ○ No advances on allowance
- Establish accountability. Parents should review their children's progress occasionally, and provide encouragement and/or redirection accordingly.
- Increase the amount of allowance as children get older. As the amount changes, review how to allocate the funds correctly. The dollar amounts shown in the following graphic are suggestions for weekly allowance; feel free to adjust the amounts to fit your budget and your needs.

How Much Allowance Should I Give My Child?

AGE 5 OR 6 - $1.00	AGE 9 - $4.00	AGE 12 - $7.00
AGE 7 - $2.00	AGE 10 - $5.00	AGE 13+ ENVELOPE SYSTEM
AGE 8 - $3.00	AGE 11 - $6.00	

The four-quarter method is easy to implement, and isn't that time consuming for parents. It creates accountability and gives rewards for good and faithful stewardship, just as the Bible teaches. As children move into middle school, a new system, the Envelope System, can build on and enhance a child's stewardship abilities.

The Envelope System (Middle School through High School)

Several years ago, I (Tim) read a book my mom had given to me called *Raising Financially Confident Kids*© by Mary Hunt (2012, Revell). This book helped me understand and develop what Life Institute, the ministry arm of our company, calls "The Envelope System". We encourage you to read this book for a much fuller treatment of the ideas presented in this section.

If you begin teaching children the principles of stewardship with the Four Quarter method, the Envelope System will build on that foundation. It teaches basic budgeting, and dives deeper into the Five Biblical Financial Priorities.

Here is how the envelope system works: When a child enters middle school, you'll help them create a budgeting plan for the coming year. For each spending category, provide them with a separate envelope labeled appropriately. Feel free to use as many envelopes as needed to help your child better allocate their income. In this system, an envelope for Long-Term Savings is important, but a separate envelope for Short-Term Savings may lack the needed clarity for your child. Essentially, most of the envelopes are a part of Short-Term savings, just on a simpler level.

With the Envelope System, income is provided monthly rather than weekly. We find it best to provide this income on the first of each month. When you pay your child, they are expected to allocate those funds into separate envelopes in anticipation of expenses over the course of the year. They'll keep track of their income by writing on envelopes or using spreadsheets.

The amount of income you give your child will depend on the kinds of expenses that will be their responsibilities. To give an example, if your daughter wants designer clothing, but it's not in your budget, allocate the amount you are willing to spend on clothing. This amount would then be included in her monthly income, allowing her to make her own spending choices. Allocating the amount may help prevent an argument or fight over clothing; just make sure the clothing budget is reasonable. It also helps to explain your rationale for the budget. The goal is for your daughter to learn the value of a dollar. She may even find creative ways to dress fashionably while on a budget.

The envelope system can be used from middle school through high school, with the amount of income and responsibility increasing each year. For example, at first, kids begin paying for expenses outside of necessities, such as youth group trips and birthday gifts for friends. Then, as they get older and begin to pay for more items and expenses, they'll divide their money into additional categories. For instance, they'll allocate amounts for cell phone bills or car insurance. Rather than paying for those things directly, you'll estimate the annual cost of those expenses, and provide the money for your child to spend on their own. This teaches them how to budget their finite resources to meet their financial priorities.

As parents, we must hold our children accountable and periodically check their progress. Be ready to encourage and redirect when needed, but also allow room for natural consequences if they don't save, or if they spend too much money.

The principles and guidelines of the four-quarter system still apply to the envelope system: always have a reserve, no borrowing, no advances, and parents will provide a matching incentive if a child's long-term savings meet or exceed the minimum expectation at the end of the year.

Continual Incentives

As parents, you can even continue incentivizing the wisdom of saving money after your kids move out of the house. There are many ways to do this, but to give an example, Roy continued to match the Russell kids' and their spouses' Roth IRA contributions up to a certain amount per person per year until they turned thirty. He also matched the contributions his grandchildren made to their college savings accounts. Roy blessed and rewarded his children and grandchildren as they demonstrated wisdom.

If this is something you'd like to do for your family, you can make this affordable and manageable by considering how much you're able to contribute. You can also think about putting an annual cap on the match amount.

Surprise Generosity

In addition to learning how to plan, save, and budget, children need to understand the importance of helping those who are less fortunate. You need to introduce your kids to the joys and rewards of giving to others.

There are many ways to go about helping others who are in need. One way the Russell family went about doing this was through the creation of a "surprise package company." One Thanksgiving, after each member of the family had shared something that they were thankful for, Roy asked us kids to think of someone we knew in our community who was in need. He explained how to keep our ears and eyes open to recognize the needs of others around us.

The reality was, as kids growing up in a Christian home and attending a Christian school, we were blind to the needs of others. Over time, we began to listen to prayer requests differently. Eventually, we identified people at school, at church, or within our community who were going through hard times and might be in need of a blessing. It was at this point that the surprise package company went into action.

The surprise package company didn't just allow the Russell kids to experience the joy of giving, we also experienced the thrill of *anonymous* giving. We identified four families to bless (one family for each Russell kid), and with our parents approval, we headed out. I (Tim) can still remember the first time I made my delivery! It was early December on a crisp Pennsylvania evening when we pulled up to the first house. We parked a house or two away from the target house. As we got closer, my dad turned the headlights off so as not to be noticed. After parking the car, my dad handed me an envelope containing $100 with a family name on it, and a piece of tape on the back. He pointed out the house I had selected. As the side door of our minivan slid open, the theme song from *Mission Impossible*© began playing in my head.

I did a dramatic front roll out of the van and made straight for a nearby tree. From there, I went from bush to tree, stopping at each one, watching and listening for signs of being caught. Before I knew it, I was at the foot of the front porch. At this point, my heart was pounding in my ears. As I placed my foot on the first wooden step, the board groaned under my weight. Gripped with the fear of being caught, I paused to see if anyone had heard the noise. The coast was clear. I ran up the steps, taped the envelope to the front door, rang the doorbell, and ran for cover. Hiding in the bushes, my heart was beating faster than ever.

Someone came to the front door. They were confused, finding no one there. Then, they noticed the envelope. With shouts of excitement and surprise, I heard, "Honey, come here! You are not going to believe this!" If you could have seen my face, you would have seen a grin as big as that house! Those are memories I will never forget. The feeling of bringing joy to others is not easily paralleled.

We understand that a surprise package company may not work for every family. Sadly, this kind of activity may be dangerous in some cultural contexts. Wisdom needs to be applied when choosing how to implement this strategy. Even if wisdom dictates a different approach, you can look for other ways to practice generosity (surprise or not) together. Also, your gift doesn't always have to be a financial one. Your family can do service projects, such as raking leaves or providing another valuable form of service. The benefit of any kind of giving is that kids will learn to be selfless in sharing their time, talents, and treasures. They'll experience the joy of giving and serving, and they'll become more and more willing to use their own resources to bless others. They'll be thankful for what they have, and by blessing others, they'll be reminded that we're all recipients of generosity through the grace of God.

Proactively Set Expectations

It's important to set expectations and help children think about their future lifestyles long before they're in a position to make major financial decisions as young adults.

My wife, Lana, and I (Roy) had a goal to help our children become wise in handling money before they entered the "real world". Teaching financial wisdom required proactively training our children on how to manage money on their own. As they became teenagers, we gave them more freedom with their money, and even allowed them to make mistakes. Our role was to advise and encourage, and if our teens happened to display a lack of financial wisdom continually, we took away some of their financial freedom and autonomy for a time. Fortunately for us, our children showed wisdom and never had to lose any of that freedom!

Once children leave home the consequences of making financial mistakes become much more significant. Don't waste the opportunity during their formative years to train them to become wise stewards of their resources.

Important Stewardship Conversations

Here are some additional ideas for how to lead stewardship conversations with your children and include real-life applications:

- Show them how to write checks and balance a checkbook.
- Include them in the creation of a family/household budget.
- Take them grocery shopping and let them compare prices/choose items.
- Ask them to help you determine how much to tithe each month.
- Show them how to use systems and technology to keep track of finances.
- At age fifteen, teach them what the Bible says about co-signing loans, and explain why you will never cosign a loan for them.
- If your kids want to get married someday, have a conversation with them about their weddings when they're sixteen. No need to discuss dollar amounts, but establish overall expectations regarding the amount you plan to contribute.

The Lasting Impact of Teaching Biblical Stewardship

Having your children help with stewardship decisions and employing methods like the envelope system prepares them to handle their finances wisely when they become adults. They'll understand and be able to apply the Five Biblical Financial Priorities. They'll be better equipped to avoid debt, and they can freely serve the church. As a result, the gospel will go forth, and the Kingdom of God will be glorified. This is a beautiful thing!

Chapter 5:

The Love of Money is a Root of All Kinds of Evil

So far, we've talked about the definition of stewardship, the cost of misaligned priorities, the Five Biblical Financial Priorities, and training the next generation to become better stewards. We've given you knowledge, along with some practical applications. There are more applications to come, but for now, it's time for us to discuss what can happen if you make money too high a priority in your lives.

Root of Evil

"For the love of money is a root of all kinds of evils. It is through this craving that some have wandered away from the faith and pierced themselves with many pangs" —*1 Timothy 6:10.*

Both Christians and non-Christians alike are familiar with these words from the book of 1 Timothy. This scripture has a much broader context than merely saying that the love of money is evil. To fully grasp what Paul is saying here, we need to understand its context, both within the chapter and within the broader book of 1 Timothy. This book of the Bible is perhaps one of the most profound and helpful books in all of Paul's writing when it comes to shaping the Christian view of money, possessions, and wealth. We will be spending the majority of our time looking at 1 Timothy 6, but let's first look at **1 Timothy 3:16.**

What Is Godliness?

"Great indeed, we confess, is the mystery of godliness"—*1 Timothy 3:16.*

The word "godliness" appears nine times within 1 Timothy, more frequently than in any other book of the Bible. What does this word mean? What does godliness entail?

Godliness includes two important and inseparable concepts: knowledge, and obedience. First, godliness requires us to have a basic knowledge or understanding of God as He is revealed to us in the Bible. Consider **Ephesians 3:18-19** where Paul prays that his readers would *"...have strength to comprehend with all the saints what is the breadth and length and height and depth, and to know the love of Christ that surpasses knowledge, that you may be filled with all the fullness of God."* Notice all the "mind" words that Paul uses. He says that we are to "comprehend" and "know" something about God. This is how we grow in godliness: by knowing God. Further, notice what Paul is praying for. He is deeply concerned with the godly character of the Ephesians. This is what is means to be *"filled with all the fullness of God."*

Knowing God doesn't mean that we've memorized the entire Bible, or that we fully understand every aspect of the faith. It means that we believe in the *core* elements of Christianity. Godliness means that we have knowledge of who Jesus is, and believe in what He accomplished for us.

Second, godliness requires obedience to the will of God. You are to live a sincere and devout life. In other words, you put into practice what you believe. Faith and life should never be separated. Godliness means that your words and your actions are largely consistent with each other.

Some may not like this idea that Godliness requires obedience, but before dismissing this truth, you must understand that no one, not even the Apostle Paul (See **Romans 7:15-25**), lived a perfectly consistent life. To be godly, one must recognize areas of inconsistency in their faith and their actions, repent of these sins, and look to Christ to finish the work of sanctification that He started in us (Phil 1:6). This is about living a *consistent* life. When you fall down, you get back up. When you make a mistake, you brush yourself off, repent, receive forgiveness from Christ, and start again.

Now that you know what it means to be godly, let's go deeper into the key verses of 1 Timothy 6.

Godliness = Gain?

"If anyone teaches a different doctrine and does not agree with the sound words of our Lord Jesus Christ and the teaching that accords with godliness, he is puffed up with conceit and understands nothing. He has an unhealthy craving for controversy and for quarrels about words... imagining that godliness is a means of gain"—1 Timothy 6:3-5.

This particular teaching from Paul about money was born from conflict with false teachers who taught that the primary benefit for godliness was wealth, or "gain". These false teachers became popular by teaching that a relationship with God could win a person significant financial gains. Sadly, their teachings were rooted in greed and *discontent*, the opposite of Paul's teaching. These false teachers wanted to grow in wealth, rather than godliness, and they viewed their relationship with God as a transaction.

This false teaching distorted God's Word, and ultimately distorted people's thoughts about the purpose of faith, life, and money. They began to seek God for money, rather than seeking God Himself. They weren't "godly" to please the Lord or to glorify Him. They adopted an unhealthy mindset, embracing religion for their own selfish reasons. And in doing so, they *failed to achieve* godliness.

When people pursue God only for the blessings they can get out of Him, they are no longer pursuing God. These people are seeking their best life now, here on this earth. Heaven is just a nice bonus. However, when one realizes their complete dependency on God, they will pursue Him with genuine faith. The Christian understands that apart from God they have nothing and deserve nothing. The Christian receives the blessings of God as an outpouring of God's love, not as a reward for obedience or devotion. The Christian finds hope and confidence in their eternal reward, and in God's present promise to meet their needs abundantly in this life.

Prosperity Gospel Misses the Mark

It's evident that Satan still attacks the church today by bringing in false teachers who seek to commercialize the Cross. They share the so-called "prosperity theology" or "prosperity gospel," spreading the false belief that earthly, material abundance should be the expectation of every committed Christian. They overvalue this life, and undervalue the life to come. This theology binds people's hearts and minds with the chains of materialism and greed. It also ignores the reality of suffering in the life of Christians (see John 16:33).

Not all godly believers have or will obtain wealth. In fact, some of the most impoverished people in the world are perhaps the most godly. While poverty itself does not create godliness, true believers who are impoverished understand that God alone can meet their needs (see Matthew 6:25-33).

Our Ultimate Goal

"But godliness with contentment is great gain…"—1 Timothy 6:6.

To be clear, Paul isn't against gain or profit. In fact, quite the opposite is true. Paul wants Timothy and the church to understand that Christians should expect "great gain." The actual word used by Paul only occurs here in 1 Timothy 6. It is a word that means "profit", "gain", or "wealth". But in this context, it's clear that he does not primarily mean material or financial wealth. He's speaking about the true wealth that comes from knowing and being known by God. Paul is saying that godliness *is* the gain. Godliness and contentment are not a means to wealth; they are the means by which we grow in our relationship with Jesus and become more Christlike. For Christians, that is the end goal.

Consider this question: can you be godly without being content? The answer is no. While godly people do struggle with discontentment from time to time, facing lack, disappointment, frustration, and wishing their situation was different, their hearts and minds won't stay there. They are able to take their eyes off their current circumstances. Their discontentment becomes an invitation to look to God instead. God has promised to be with them, transforming suffering into good in their lives.

St. Augustine says in his *Confessions, "You have made us for yourself, O Lord, and our hearts are restless until they rest in You."* Contentment comes when we come face to face with the living God. Contentment is possible when we trust in His goodness to meet our needs. If He's not the foundation and anchor of our faith and contentment, then we'll constantly seek to fill that void with something else. But when we find our joy and contentment in Christ, we become unshakeable. No hardship or suffering will take our eyes off our good God.

Riches are Temporary

"For we brought nothing into the world, and we cannot take anything out of the world"—1 Timothy 6:7.

After Paul talks about godliness and contentment while we're on earth in verse 6, he presents us with the eternal perspective in verse 7. Since we brought nothing into this world, and we can't take anything out of it, aren't materialism and greed foolish? Paul clearly demonstrates this point by talking about the finite nature of life.

I heard a sermon illustration once that has always stuck with me. Imagine you're holding the end of a rope in your right hand, which stretches all the way around the earth until its other end is in your left hand. That's a pretty long rope! Now, as you look at the rope in your hand, you notice a small dot made with a permanent marker on one end. That dot represents your life here on Earth. The rope is just a fraction of your life throughout eternity. We tend to focus all of our energy on making that dot the best dot it can be, with little or no thought about the rest of the rope.

The reality of eternity should have at least three significant influences on the good steward. First, you realize the foolishness of seeking to maximize your status and comfort in this life. Second, you delight in using your resources to fund kingdom ministries, thus storing up treasures in heaven. You find that doing so maximizes Your joy in this life, both for yourself and for others. Finally, you proactively train up the next generation of stewards to follow in your footsteps as you follow Christ. When you train the next generation to be good stewards, you can leave this world knowing they're prepared to wisely manage what you'll leave behind. We'll discuss how you can best decide who will be the next steward of your assets in Chapter 9.

Directing Our Desires

"But those who desire to be rich fall into temptation, into a snare, into many senseless and harmful desires that plunge people into ruin and destruction"—1 Timothy 6:9.

The word "desire" is not a sinful word, and desires aren't necessarily a bad thing. In fact, Paul uses this word earlier in his letter for positive desires (**1 Tim 2:8 & 5:14**). In this context, however, the desire itself is sinful because the desire is an all-consuming passion for more. While not addressing this passage in particular, pastor and author John Piper's definition of sinful desire is helpful. According to his definition, a desire becomes sinful when a) the object of desire is impure, or b) the desire is so strong that it disorders our thoughts, feelings, and actions.[6] Clearly, this is what Paul has in mind.

Paul warns that because of its default condition, the human heart will run into problems when obtaining wealth or possessions becomes a controlling motivation. We tend to romanticize wealth and think about all the wonderful things we can do or experience if only we had more money. We rarely consider the toll that the acquisition of wealth can have on overall contentment, relationships, faith, and genuine happiness.

---

[6] Piper, John, "What is Lust?" Desiring God, https://www.youtube.com/watch?v=GQ-tC_SpM34

The Love of Money is a Root of all Kinds of Evil

Those who make it their aim to become wealthy often find increased pain and misery. However, wealth is not evil, and money is not bad. God created wealth and money, and when used His way, money and wealth can accomplish much good in this world. But when the pursuit of wealth becomes a driving force in our lives, pain may be just around the corner.

Notice in this passage that ruin and destruction don't happen immediately; they follow a progression. First, we are tempted. The allure of money and possessions can sink deep into our heart, causing us to become discontent with our car, home, job, and possessions. I know we've said this already, but it's worth repeating. At the root of discontentment is a lack of trust in the goodness of God, and in all that He has provided or promises to provide. We want heaven and all of its joys here and now, because we aren't content to wait for future fulfillment.

Second, we fall right into Satan's trap, having become discontent with our lot in life. Paul uses the word "snare," which is a kind of trap typically used to catch birds, making it impossible for them to get away. The same Greek word was used of the Trojan Horse,[7] which the citizens of Troy embraced, but only brought about their destruction.

Finally, discontentment and an insatiable desire for wealth lead to senseless and harmful desires that *plunge us into ruin and destruction*. Again, this verse is telling us that destruction is a downward spiral—we don't find ourselves in ruin and destruction all of a sudden. Temptation, a snare, and senseless and harmful desires lead us there little by little. Before we know it, we find our lives in tatters and our faith (if it ever existed) hanging on by a thread. In these verses, you have learned that those whose hearts are captured by wealth (or the pursuit of it) ultimately get the opposite of what they desire. Instead of wealth, they end up in ruin and destruction. You must guard your hearts from the love of money.

---

[7] δουρατέα π., of the Trojan horse, AP9.152 (Agath.) Henry George Liddell et al., A Greek-English Lexicon (Oxford: Clarendon Press, 1996), 1284.

Resist Temptation

In **Timothy 6:9**, Paul states that we *fall* into temptation. This means that temptation usually comes to us externally, but there are internal temptations, too.

In his book, *Temptations: Resisted and Repulsed*, (2018, Banner of Truth) Puritan author and pastor John Owen (1616-1683) says that falling into temptation is different from experiencing the *test* of temptation. The way we react to temptation can't be neutral or passive. We must avoid the circumstances and settings where we often meet temptation. If temptation can't be prevented, then at the earliest opportunity, we must flee from its presence. David was called "a man after God's own heart" and yet he committed adultery and murder. Are you stronger and wiser than David? If David could fall into temptation, how much more likely is it for us to fall if we do not keep careful watch? "Therefore let anyone who thinks that he stands take heed lest he fall." **1 Corinthians 10:12**

Finally, if we can't avoid or flee from temptation, then we must fight temptation with God's help and power by putting on the Armor of God (**Eph 6:10-18**).

If you struggle with the allure of wealth, you should avoid people, places, websites, TV shows, and other forms of media that evoke this desire. Read **Ephesians 1** or **Romans 8** to remind you of all that God has promised to those who trust in Him and wait patiently for his return.

The Root of Evil

"For the love of money is a root of all kinds of evils. It is through this craving that some have wandered away from the faith and pierced themselves with many pangs"—1 Timothy 6:10

Finally, we return to the verse from the beginning of the chapter, the one that is most familiar to us. To better understand this verse, we need to examine its various parts to see how they fit together. The phrase *"the love of money"* points to the greedy pursuit of wealth. God made money; therefore it is not, in and of itself, evil. Yet when it becomes the primary object of our love, we may do unspeakable evils to get it and keep it. This is far beyond the natural desire to meet one's needs. Paul used the negative of this phrase, "not a lover of money" to describe the character of elders (**1 Tim 3:3**). We can see that those who love money are violating God's first commandment to "have no other gods before me" (**Exodus 20:3**).

Next, consider the word *"root."* For a plant, the root serves at least two key functions. First, the root feeds vital nutrients to the plant. Second, it supports and stabilizes the plant against wind and rain. Loving money acts as a root in that it feeds evil desires, and it deceives people to pursue their own pleasures no matter the cost. Further, it prevents us from feeling the need for change and repentance. Perhaps this is why Jesus said it is more difficult for a rich man to enter the kingdom of God than for a camel to go through the eye of a needle. (**Luke 18:25**)

The phrase *"all kinds of evil"* is instructive. First, we must note that loving money isn't the source of every evil. There are great evils that have nothing to do with money. For instance, when Cain killed his brother Abel (**Gen 4**), it was not about money. Yet almost every evil act can be intensified by the love of money.

The word *"craving"* is an interesting choice, and it's not necessarily a negative word. In fact, Paul previously used the same root word for craving to describe the healthy desire to (*"aspires to"*) become an elder in **1 Tim 3:1**. Yet it is clear in the context of **1 Tim 6:10** that Paul is not referring to a natural or positive desire. He's talking about an all-consuming pursuit.

The words *"wandered away from the faith,"* point to the sad trajectory of those who love money. Rather than seeking Christ and growing in their relationship with Him, they wander from the faith in pursuit of temporary riches which are lost after death. Jesus tells us that *"no one can serve two masters, for either he will hate the one and love the other, or he will be devoted to the one and despise the other. You cannot serve God and money."* (**Matt 6:24**).

Finally, *"pierced themselves with many pangs,"* shows us the destiny of all who make wealth their god. Having rejected God in the pursuit of riches, those who love money receive the opposite of what they sought. Those who give in to temptation pierce themselves with many pangs. This pain is *self-inflicted*, and they have no one to blame but themselves.

Trusting God's Promises When We Don't Have "Enough"

Oftentimes, our hearts believe the lies of Satan. The Devil says, "God won't provide enough. Your financial success depends on you. You shouldn't rely on God, He doesn't really love you." Our enemy is a skilled deceiver. We must be on our guard against his lies.

The best way to combat Satan's lies is to preach and claim the precious promises of God. One such promise is found in **Philippians 4:19**, *"And my God will supply every need of yours according to his riches in glory in Christ Jesus."* When you are tempted to believe the lies, go back to the truth, and pray over the truth. Ask God to be faithful to His Word and meet your needs. Notice this verse in Philippians tells us that God gives us what we *need*, not necessarily what we *want*. Discontentment arises in our hearts when we distrust the goodness of God.

What happens when we don't feel that we have enough? Does this mean that God has failed to keep His promises? By no means! Consider **Romans 8:18**: *"For I consider that the sufferings of this present time are not worth comparing with the glory that is to be revealed to us (in heaven)."* In **verse 28,** Paul continues by saying, *"And we know that for those who love God all things work together for good, for those who are called according to his purpose."* God may use times of suffering or scarcity to show us His sufficiency and goodness. Can we trust God to give us what we need? Yes, and that is a promise worth building your life upon.

By Faith, Through Grace

In reading this chapter, maybe you've become aware that you've been trying to use God for your own gain, or that you still have greed or distrust in your heart. The human soul was not created to find contentment in the accumulation of "stuff." Unfortunately, some people still chase money and possessions, which robs them of the peace that can only be found in an intimate relationship with God.

As Christians, we can't be good stewards on our own. We don't have enough power, faith, goodness, or virtue within ourselves to be godly. We must remember that God enables us to do the works He has called us to do, through His grace. Instead of leaning on ourselves, we lean on Christ, and in doing so, good stewardship happens by virtue of the Holy spirit working within us by faith, through grace. This is the mystery and the beauty of the Christian faith.

Grace must be at the forefront of our lives; otherwise, there's no way we're going to find true success. When we look back at Haggai 1, God calls people out on their sin, and after they repent, God enables them to do what He called them to do. He wasn't going to crush them; He was going to help them.

I'll Never Leave You

"Keep your life free from the love of money, and be content with what you have because God has said, "I will never leave you nor forsake you" —Hebrews 13:5.

As we conclude this chapter, we want to give you one more reason to make Christ your greatest desire and pursuit. The author of Hebrews reminds his audience that God has promised to be with those who trust in His name through all of life's ups and downs. He will not leave us when the going gets tough. He will not forsake us when we disappoint Him and rebel against Him. This is yet another reason why we can trust God in all circumstances!

God is not a means to an end (i.e., more stuff); He *is* the end. We seek to be good stewards because *He* matters, and we value Him more than we do our possessions. We begin to pursue Him instead of money, because we believe He will never leave us or forsake us. This is a rock-solid promise.

In the next chapter, we'll look at the second half of **1 Timothy 6** to learn what God expects from those who have wealth. The answer may surprise you.

Chapter 6:

Redefining Wealth

In the previous chapter, we considered Paul's warning in **1 Timothy 6:3-10** about the sinful desire to be rich, which prioritizes acquiring wealth before building a relationship with God. We have seen the destructive results of greed. In this chapter, we'll continue to consider Paul's words, but our focus will be on his prescription in **1 Timothy 6:17-19,** for those who are already rich. Is wealth always destructive, or are there ways to use wealth to honor God and serve others? To make that determination, we first need to answer the question, "Who is already wealthy?"

Who Is Rich/Wealthy?
"As for the rich in this present age…" —1 Timothy 6:17.

You may be thinking, "OK, I get it. Don't love money. But what about those who already have it? What should they do?" Paul anticipated this question, and his answer is found in **vs 17-19**. Here we read the words, "…as for the rich in this present age," and instantly, we breathe a huge sigh of relief because we know Paul is not talking about us. We don't have infinite resources, live in a mansion, or cruise around in a yacht. We aren't rich. Clearly, Paul has someone else in mind, right?

Paul clarifies in **1 Timothy 6:8** what he has in mind: *"But if we have food and clothing, with these we will be content."* This helps us to see and understand that part of what it means to be wealthy in Paul's mind is to have more than the basic necessities of life. Most of you who are reading this book have food in your pantries and clothes in your closets. You have a roof over your heads, cars to drive, bank accounts to hold some of your money, and many people reading this book even have retirement accounts.

The truth is, if you have food, clothing, a vehicle, and a roof over your head, you have more wealth than the majority of other people on this planet.

Many of us see the mansions and yachts of the billionaires and think that compared to them we're not rich. Rather than comparing ourselves to the wealthiest person on earth, it might be more helpful to compare ourselves to the *average* person. At the risk of becoming outdated quickly, at the time of publication the average global household income was $12,235 per year[8]. If you could afford the purchase of this book, you are probably wealthier than the majority of the rest of the world.

When you recognize your wealth on a global scale, you can better understand how blessed you are with all that God has provided. In a recent global wealth report[9], you'll learn the following:

- If you have $10,000 worth of "stuff," such as bank accounts, cars, and clothing, you're among the top 52.5 percent of wealthiest people on the planet.
- If you have $100,000, you're among the top 13 percent of the richest people in the world.
- If you have $1,000,000, you're in the top 1 percent.
- If you earned $35,000 last year, you're among the top 5 percent of paid workers in the world.

According to this report, Americans are incredibly wealthy by all comparison.

---

[8] https://www.zippia.com/advice/average-income-worldwide/

[9] The report can be accessed at the address below and the information is found on page 22 of the report. https://www.ubs.com/global/en/family-office-uhnw/reports/global-wealth-report-2023.html

Discussing the wealth and income gap between you and the majority of the rest of the world is not meant to shame you. Rather, we bring it up to help you recalibrate your definition of wealth. By doing this, we find that Paul's words to the rich in **1 Timothy 6** apply to more of us than expected. Paul is not just talking to the millionaires and billionaires of the world. He's talking to us and to you.

Paul's Prescription for the Rich

So, if you and I are whom Paul considers to be "the rich in this present age," what are we supposed to do? How do we keep ourselves free from the love of money? How do we use our wealth for the glory of God? Let's look at **1 Timothy 6:17-19** to see what Paul has to say about the matter.

To be clear, the word "rich" is not meant to be negative. Paul does not think that all "rich" people are lazy, selfish, and cold-hearted. For example, Joseph of Arimathea was a man who used his riches to provide the tomb for Jesus' body after the crucifixion. King David and King Solomon were also extremely wealthy. David was considered a man after God's own heart, and Solomon was one of the wisest men to ever live. Clearly, riches are not bad. Rather, they have the power for great good.

In **1 Timothy 6:17-19**, Paul offers five prescriptions for how the rich can honor God with their wealth. The first two prescriptions discuss the things we are to *stop* doing. The last three prescriptions discuss what we are to *start* doing. These ideas are similar to others Paul presents elsewhere in his writings (see **Ephesians 4:22-24**) about "putting off" a particular action or thought pattern, while at the same time "putting on" other new thoughts or actions. These prescriptions are also based on the two greatest commandments.

Prescription 1: Don't be Prideful
"...charge them not to be haughty..."
—1 Timothy 6:17

The Bible teaches that God knows the heart of man: *"I the Lord search the heart and test the mind..."* (**Jeremiah 17:10**). Because He does this, He understands how wealth can cause our hearts to grow proud.

Prideful hearts cause us to look down on those who have less than we do. It's too easy to look down on others who live in smaller homes; drive older, more beat up vehicles, or work menial jobs. Pride is toxic to the culture and mission of the Church.

To give a specific example, in **1 Corinthians 11:17-22**, Paul addresses abuses that occurred at the Lord's Table. The rich were gorging themselves on the best of the food, leaving little to nothing for those who were poor. In **Philippians 2:3-4**, Paul says, *"Do nothing from selfish ambition or conceit, but in humility count others as more significant than yourselves. Let each of you look not only to his own interests, but also to the interests of others."* We could go on and on discussing different texts that address the issue of pride, but for now, let's simply acknowledge that pride is a significant sin.

In **1 Timothy 6:17,** Paul uses the word "haughty" to describe the attitude of the rich that needs to come to an end. We are not to be arrogant, selfish, or pompously egotistic when it comes to our wealth. People who earn less than you *are not less than you.* In fact, there is much that the wealthy can learn from those who have less, such as contentment, peace, faith in God to meet their needs, and finding joy in the little things of life.

When you start to think you are the source and cause of all your success, you have entered dangerous ground. Whatever blessings you have or success you have achieved comes from God. When you take credit for what God has done, you dishonor Him and harm yourself. However, when you view all of your success and possessions as a completely undeserved gift from God, you become free to use your wealth in worship of Him and service to others.

Prescription 2: Don't Trust in Your Wealth
"…nor to set their hopes on the uncertainty of riches…"
—*1 Timothy 6:17.*

Our pride causes us to only trust in what we can see and touch. If we see ourselves as the ones who made our wealth possible, then we're going to attach our feelings of safety and security to our wealth. This means that when things are going well, when the economy is hot, and the stock market is rising, we can feel bulletproof. We think nothing in the world can hold us back. But when the economy weakens, we lose our job, or our portfolio takes a big hit, our confidence ebbs like the tide leaving the shore. This is why Christians are called to stop hoping in the uncertainty of riches. They are temporary and insecure at best. Rather than trusting in God whose steadfast love endures forever (see **Psalm 136**), we tend to trust in wealth and possessions that are here today and gone tomorrow. If you place all of your hope in money and suddenly it's gone, where do you turn? Where then, do you place your hope?

The Test

How can you tell if you've put your hope in the uncertainty of riches? Ask yourself the following questions:

How do I feel when the economy enters a recession?

- What happens in my heart when I learn of layoffs coming to my company?
- How do you I when I have a significant unexpected expense or when my spouse doesn't follow the budget?
- When the stock market drops, do I become more anxious about the future?
- Do I feel more secure and confident when the stock market is performing well?
- When my retirement account balances are lower than expected, do I get upset?
- Do I feel safer when my retirement account balances are growing?

If you answered yes to any of these questions, use God's Word to renew your mind and rest in His peace. Don't let the amount of money in your accounts be your security. Let God be your security!

Prescription 3: Trust In God

"...but [set your hopes] on God, who richly provides us with everything to enjoy..." —*1 Timothy 6:17.*

It's not enough to just stop doing the wrong things. You need to replace old thoughts or actions with new ones. Not only do you need to stop trusting in yourself and your wealth, but you also must start trusting in God. This may go without saying, but it's critical for you to put this into practice. You are to place your hope in God. The word "hope" means a firm expectation, a confidence in the trustworthiness and reliability of that in which you hope. Therefore, placing your *hope* in God is *trusting* in God.

Why should you trust in God? Paul offers several compelling reasons in his text. You can trust in God because He *"richly provides us with everything to enjoy."* Let's break this down.

First, your God is rich, not a penny pinching miser. When He meets a need, He does so out of His abundance. It's no struggle for God to bless you. After all, He owns the cattle on a thousand hills (**Psalm 50:10**). Not only that, but God also blesses "richly," which means that He blesses you in ways far better than you deserve.

Second, notice that it is God who provides. When you credit your own efforts, wisdom, or work ethic for your wellbeing, your confidence can easily be shaken by sickness, layoffs, or other frustrations. However, when you understand that God is the true provider, you can face all manner of difficulties and frustrations with confidence that He will continue to provide.

Third, God cares about your joy. Every blessing given by God is meant to increase your joy and happiness. You are not meant to find joy in the abundance of your possessions, but in the generosity and kindness of the gift giver. You must not allow joy from the material blessings of God to replace your joy in Him and His goodness. The fact that God cares about your joy also indicates that it's not wrong to be rich, or to have nice things. Neither the rich nor the poor have special standing before God based on their wealth. Compared with God, both the "rich" and the "poor" are wretchedly pitiful and impoverished (**Revelation 3:17**).

Prescription 4: Be Rich in Good Works

"They are to do good, to be rich in good works..."—*1 Timothy 6:18.*

In **Matthew 22:34-40**, Jesus explains the two greatest commandments: love God with all that we are, and love our neighbor as ourselves. From this we learn that it's impossible to have true love for God and not have it result in having greater concern for others, so following the first commandment results in us following the second. In this passage in **1 Timothy 6:18**, Paul uses two verbs, "do good" and "be rich" to describe the good steward. These two verbs help us see that loving God with all our heart, soul, mind, and strength will change the way we engage with those around us in two ways.

First, it will change your actions. You will "do good." This means you will use your wealth to help others, rather than maximize your own luxurious lifestyle. You are to view your wealth as a means of setting yourself free to do good things for others. This may include taking time off from work to help someone in need, or using your resources to meet the needs of others. For example, you might spend your summer vacation on a mission or service trip.

Second, it will change your identity. You will "be rich in good works." Generally, those who are rich want to be known as wealthy. Their identity can be wrapped up in the clothes they wear or the things they possess. However, the good steward understands the need for a new identity. God is rich toward us in how He provides everything to enjoy, and Paul wants those who have experienced God's generosity to be defined by their generosity toward others. The idea behind "be rich in good works" means much more than just making a donation to the poor; it implies that the rich are to actually get involved in the work.

When you're rich in good works, it helps you develop an eternal perspective about money. Being rich in good works doesn't mean you occasionally do good; it means that good works are a regular part of your everyday behavior. We should go through life open-handed, not with closed fists. Open hands seek to bless others, and are ready to receive blessings from the Lord.

A word of caution: as we talk about good works, we aren't saying that the rich (or anyone for that matter) can earn God's favor by doing them. We can't compensate for past failures by doing good or being generous. What God wants is for us to turn to Him in repentance and faith. We are to seek His forgiveness, which is based on His grace, not the amount of good we have done. Good works do not increase our favor with God—they naturally flow out of a heart that has been changed by God's grace (**Ephesians 2:8-10**).

Prescription 5: Be Generous Toward Others
"…to be generous and ready to share…" —*1 Timothy 6:18.*

The last prescription Paul gives is to be generous. In the Greek, he uses two adjectives to describe what doing good looks like. The first word is translated "generous," which means to share liberally or to freely give. Some of us are concerned that our gifts to the poor will be spent on drugs or alcohol. This fear causes some to never give to people on the street. While this concern is understandable, it can cause us to close our ears to the cries of the poor (**Proverbs 21:13**). While there is a time and place to give to those on the street, we encourage a more relational approach to helping the poor. Therefore, we encourage you to find people in your church and community who are in need of help or encouragement, and be a part of God's plan to meet their needs.

Consider the following texts:

- *"If a brother or sister is poorly clothed and lacking in daily food, and one of you says to them, "Go in peace, be warmed and filled," without giving them the things needed for the body, what good is that?"* **James 2:15–16.**

- *"But if anyone has the world's goods and sees his brother in need, yet closes his heart against him, how does God's love abide in him? Little children, let us not love in word or talk but in deed and in truth"* **1 John 3:17–18.**

The second word used by Paul to describe what doing good looks like is translated "ready to share." In Greek, this is a form of the word *koinonia*, the word that is often translated to mean "fellowship." When we share our belongings with others, we enter into a beautiful form of fellowship with them. And when we believe that God shares His wealth with us, we can be free to share our belongings with others.

While we are called to give, generosity also requires wisdom. There have been many well-intentioned people who do more harm than good when seeking to help those in need. As referenced in chapter 3, the book *When Helping Hurts: How to Alleviate Poverty Without Hurting Yourself Or Others*© (2014, Corbett, Fikkert, & Platt, Moody Publishers) is particularly helpful when considering working with and serving the poor, and we really believe that this book is crucial for helping the poor effectively.

Result of the Five Prescriptions

"…thus storing up treasure for themselves as a good foundation for the future, so that they may take hold of that which is truly life"—1 Timothy 6:19.

Some object to generosity, thinking, "When I give to others, there is less for me. If I have $100 and give $25 away, I'll only have $75 left." The problem with this perspective is that it assumes your needs will be satisfied by *your* work and effort, rather than by God. But if you sacrifice for others, you are truly serving God. This objection does not take God at His word when He says in **Luke 6:38**, *"…give, and it will be given to you. Good measure, pressed down, shaken together, running over, will be put into your lap. For with the measure you use it will be measured back to you."* We are convinced that God will give to you if He knows that He can give *through* you.

God always rewards those who are generous. We've considered that blessings may very well come in the form of material rewards here on earth. This is confirmed in many passages throughout Scripture, but we must not limit our expectation of God's blessings to only be earthly or material things. The best rewards are those we will have for all eternity.

1 Timothy 6:19 teaches us that when the rich follow these five prescriptions, they do something of inestimable eternal value. Rather than depleting their resources, they are storing them up for the future. In fact, we are told that these works are a "good foundation for the future." However, this does not mean that good works and generosity will secure salvation. Rather, they are investments toward eternal rewards.

When we consider the objection given above through the perspective of this verse, we recognize that when we have $100 and give away $25, we are left with $75 on earth, but we'll have something infinitely more valuable than $25 in the treasury of heaven. The gift of $25 is not an expense, but an investment in eternity. This is the meaning of "storing up treasure for themselves as a good foundation for the future."

When we are freed from the love of money and seek to use what God has entrusted to us for the good of others, we are able to "take hold" of something that has far greater value, namely, a full life found in Christ alone. Those who are the most generous with their time, energy, and resources will have the richest, most joyful lives now and for all eternity.

Conclusion

As you process the five prescriptions for the rich (i.e., you and me) let's consider the life and ministry of missionary Jim Elliot (October 8, 1927–January 8, 1956). He died in Ecuador at the hands of the Aucas/Waodani tribe, whom he was trying to reach with the Gospel. He was only 29 when he was martyred. Jim knew he could spend his entire life accumulating possessions in an attempt to protect and improve his life, but in the end, he would still die like everyone else. This realization led him to write the following in his journal a month before his death: "He is no fool who gives what he cannot keep to gain that which he cannot lose." Do you believe that there is a treasure you can't lose? If so, how do your choices in life reflect this belief? Do your financial and charitable activities reflect this as well?

As you recognize your own relative wealth and God's charge for you to trust in Him and do good, consider giving more than a tithe. If God has richly blessed you, look for opportunities to be rich in good works and to put His wealth back into circulation. No amount of effort or money spent for God in service to others will go unrewarded.

Chapter 7:

Growing God's Wealth

On one hand, we've learned the good steward views wealth as God's, and it must be used to further His priorities. He is generous and ready to share. The good steward does not find his ultimate worth and value in the assets entrusted to him, but in his relationship with God, the giver of all good gifts.

On the other hand, the good steward seeks to wisely maintain and grow that which has been entrusted to him. He invests and saves in order to follow biblical calls for wisdom and prudence. But how do these truths fit together? How can we possibly be both generous and thrifty, store treasures in heaven, and save for retirement? How can we manage and invest God's wealth without becoming controlled by that wealth? The rest of this book answers this apparent dilemma.

Biblical Foundation for Saving and Investing

We've already addressed saving in chapter 3. In this chapter, we'll go deeper into this financial priority, helping you gain a much fuller perspective on what God expects of His children.

Save… Because We Live in a Fallen World

"Count it all joy, my brothers, when you meet trials of various kinds…" —James 1:2.

Notice the text says "when," not "if" trials come. The good steward is not surprised when trials come his way. Rather than viewing life through "rose colored glasses," you must see the world as it really

112

is. If you don't take a sober approach to reality, you will take your eyes off God when things are going well, and also when life seems to be falling apart.

In chapter 3, we described how science and theology agree that things break and wear out. Ultimately, life in a world impacted by the fall (**Genesis 3**) is what causes these frustrations. If you ignore this fact, you will have difficulty avoiding debt when the roof leaks or the tires on your car wear out. Having reserves is not necessarily a sign of a lack of trust in God (although as discussed earlier, that's what it can become). Reserves are a sign of trusting God and taking Him at His Word. God tells us that we will experience trials, and we are expected to proactively prepare to meet those troubles. The bottom line is that the good steward is not surprised when things break and need to be replaced.

Save… Because the Good Steward is Proactive

"The prudent sees danger and hides himself, but the simple go on and suffer for it" —Proverbs 22:3 & 27:12.

The good steward looks ahead, and is prepared with reserves. He considers upcoming possibilities and expenses, and he is proactive, not reactive. If you recall, Joseph is a prime example of a wise steward who stored up reserves. In **Genesis 41**, God showed him that Egypt would experience seven years of plenty then seven years of famine. By storing up reserves during the years of plenty, Joseph prepared the nation for the years of scarcity.

Save… Because the Good Steward is wise

"Precious treasure and oil are in a wise man's dwelling, but a foolish man devours it" —Proverbs 21:20.

The word "devour" is particularly instructive. It is the same word used in the book of Jonah to describe how a great fish swallowed up .the prophet. Far too many people live paycheck to paycheck, having no reserves. Do you devour or spend all of your income and put nothing into savings? Is this a sign of wisdom or foolishness?

When we teach this verse in our seminars, we emphasize the word "wise" as opposed to "rich", because people tend to assume that only the rich have stores or reserves. However, it's really the *wise* who have reserves. It's the fool who lives paycheck to paycheck, never making an attempt to save or grow their wealth. So, having reserves is not a sign of wealth; it's a sign of wisdom. And this wisdom often *leads to* wealth.

Why Invest?

Investing rewards those who have a long-term perspective, but today, most people want fast results. We live in a world of fast food and next day (or even same day) delivery. If we want something, we want it now. The concept of delayed gratification seems to be foreign nowadays. Yet, the principle of investing for a long period of time, which can yield potentially significant growth, has never been more relevant.

Investing is not just for the super-rich. It's not something that only those who love money should do, and it's not just for those with extremely high risk tolerances. Investing is for normal people, like you and me.

The "Magic" of Compound Interest

We have no doubt that you have heard stories of people investing a relatively small amount of money in a stock or another investment, which decades later was worth many times the amount originally invested. How can this be true? How does a small investment grow into a potentially significant one? This is where the "magic" of compound interest comes into play.

Compound interest requires two ingredients: money and time. The more money you invest, the greater the potential growth. The longer the time period that the money is invested, the greater the potential growth. Another component of success involves consistently investing month after month, year after year, in both good and bad markets. Successful investors stick to their plan regardless of market direction. Being consistent also implies that you have an investing plan, and/or you're working with a financial advisor regularly to make sure that your plan is still sound.

Someone who puts money in the market one month and hopes for it to grow because he needs it next month is not investing...he's gambling. Since 1980, the stock market has had a positive return 75% of the time, or 32 out of 43 years. If one invests consistently for ten years, there is a 99% chance of a positive return on your investment. See the following charts for reference.

Annual returns and intra-year declines

S&P intra-year declines vs. calendar year returns
Despite average intra-year drops of 14.1%, annual returns were positive in 34 of 45 years

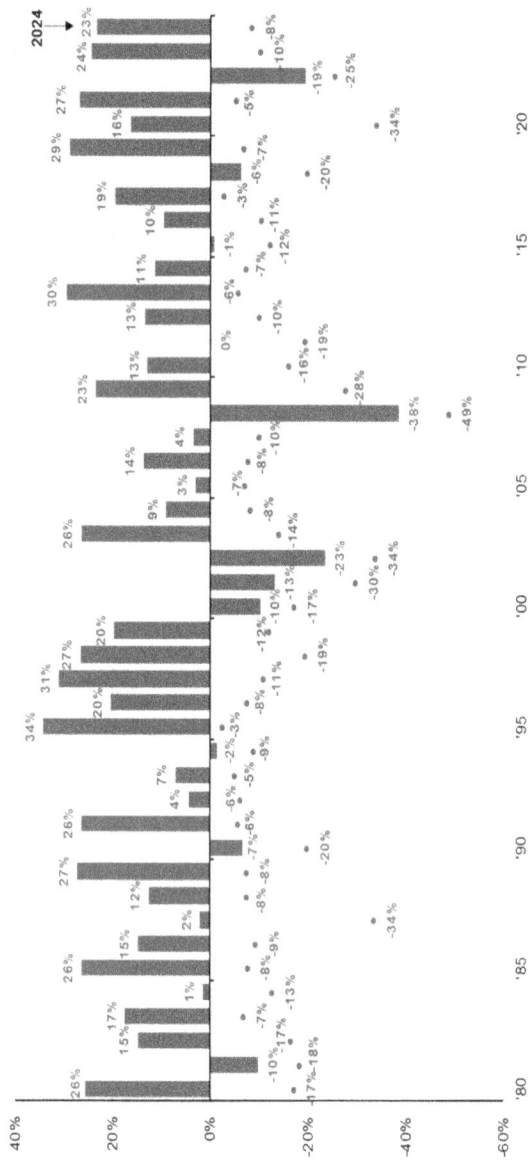

Source: FactSet, Standard & Poor's, J.P. Morgan Asset Management.
Returns are based on price index only and do not include dividends. Intra-year drops refers to the largest market drops from a peak to a trough during the year. For illustrative purposes only. Returns shown are calendar year returns from 1980 to 2024, over which time period the average annual return was 10.4%.
Guide to the Markets – U.S. Data are as of December 31, 2024.

J.P.Morgan
ASSET MANAGEMENT

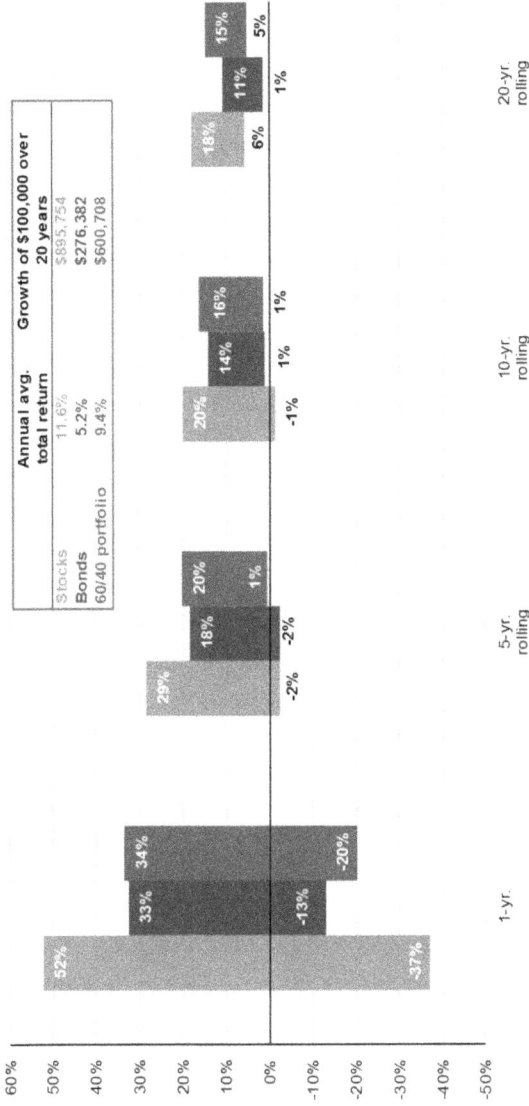

Time, diversification and the volatility of returns

Range of stock, bond and blended total returns
Annual total returns, 1950–2024

	Annual avg. total return	Growth of $100,000 over 20 years
Stocks	11.6%	$895,754
Bonds	5.2%	$276,382
60/40 portfolio	9.4%	$600,708

1-yr. 52% / 34% / 33% / -13% / -20% / -37%

5-yr. rolling 29% / 20% / 18% / 1% / -2% / -2%

10-yr. rolling 20% / 16% / 14% / 1% / 1% / -1%

20-yr. rolling 18% / 15% / 11% / 6% / 5% / 1%

Source: Bloomberg, FactSet, Federal Reserve, Standard & Poor's, Strategas/Ibbotson, J.P. Morgan Asset Management. Returns shown are based on calendar year returns from 1950 to 2024. Bonds represent Strategas/Ibbotson for periods prior to 1976 and the Bloomberg Aggregate thereafter. Growth of $100,000 is based on annual average total returns from 1950 to 2024.
Guide to the Markets – U.S. Data are as of December 31, 2024.

GTM U.S. 63

J.P.Morgan
ASSET MANAGEMENT

Investing Principles

63

So, what is compound interest? It's when the interest earned from an investment is added to the principal amount. Essentially, the interest earns interest. This is beneficial because it allows the growth of an investment to grow. In other words, if you keep an investment for a long period of time, the magnitude of growth can be so significant that the original amount invested pales in comparison.

The Magic of Compound Interest

Age	Investor A		Investor B		Investor C		Investor D	
	Invest	Year-End Value	Invest	Year-End Value	Invest	Year-End Value	Invest	Year-End Value
8	$0	$0	$0	$0	$0	$0	$2,400	$2,592
9	$0	$0	$0	$0	$0	$0	$2,400	$5,391
10	$0	$0	$0	$0	$0	$0	$2,400	$8,415
11	$0	$0	$0	$0	$2,400	$2,640	$2,400	$11,680
12	$0	$0	$0	$0	$2,400	$5,544	$2,400	$15,206
13	$0	$0	$0	$0	$2,400	$8,580	$2,400	$19,015
14	$0	$0	$0	$0	$2,400	$11,858	$0	$20,536
15	$0	$0	$0	$0	$2,400	$15,399	$0	$22,179
16	$0	$0	$0	$0	$2,400	$19,222	$0	$23,953
17	$0	$0	$0	$0	$2,400	$23,352	$0	$25,869
18	$0	$0	$2,400	$2,592	$2,400	$27,812	$0	$27,939
19	$0	$0	$2,400	$5,391	$0	$30,037	$0	$30,174
20	$0	$0	$2,400	$8,415	$0	$32,440	$0	$32,588
21	$0	$0	$2,400	$11,680	$0	$35,036	$0	$35,195
22	$2,400	$2,592	$2,400	$15,206	$0	$37,838	$0	$38,011
23	$2,400	$5,391	$2,400	$19,015	$0	$40,865	$0	$41,051
24	$2,400	$8,415	$2,400	$23,128	$0	$44,135	$0	$44,335
25	$2,400	$11,680	$2,400	$27,570	$0	$47,665	$0	$47,882
26	$2,400	$15,206	$2,400	$32,368	$0	$51,479	$0	$51,713
27	$2,400	$19,015	$2,400	$37,549	$0	$55,597	$0	$55,850
28	$2,400	$23,128	$2,400	$43,145	$0	$60,045	$0	$60,318

These are hypothetical scenarios based on the stated contribution amounts and an assumed annual 8% rate of return with no withdrawals over the life of the account. The numbers stated do not reflect any particular investment and are not implying any guarantee that you will experience the same result. Past performance of any investment cannot be assumed or guaranteed into the future. With any investment, consider any and all objectives, risks, sales charges and expenses before investing.

Age	Investor A		Investor B		Investor C		Investor D	
36	$2,400	$70,378	$2,400	$107,429	$0	$111,139	$0	$111,644
37	$2,400	$78,601	$2,400	$118,615	$0	$120,030	$0	$120,576
38	$2,400	$87,481	$2,400	$130,696	$0	$129,632	$0	$130,222
39	$2,400	$97,071	$2,400	$143,744	$0	$140,003	$0	$140,640
40	$2,400	$107,429	$2,400	$157,835	$0	$151,203	$0	$151,891
41	$2,400	$118,615	$0	$170,462	$0	$163,299	$0	$164,042
42	$2,400	$130,696	$0	$184,099	$0	$176,363	$0	$177,165
43	$2,400	$143,744	$0	$198,827	$0	$190,472	$0	$191,339
44	$2,400	$157,835	$0	$214,733	$0	$205,710	$0	$206,646
45	$2,400	$173,054	$0	$231,912	$0	$222,167	$0	$223,177
46	$2,400	$189,491	$0	$250,465	$0	$239,940	$0	$241,032
47	$2,400	$207,242	$0	$270,502	$0	$259,135	$0	$260,314
48	$2,400	$226,413	$0	$292,142	$0	$279,866	$0	$281,139
49	$2,400	$247,118	$0	$315,514	$0	$302,256	$0	$303,630
50	$2,400	$269,480	$0	$340,755	$0	$326,436	$0	$327,921
51	$2,400	$293,630	$0	$368,015	$0	$352,551	$0	$354,155
52	$2,400	$319,712	$0	$397,456	$0	$380,755	$0	$382,487
53	$2,400	$347,881	$0	$429,253	$0	$411,215	$0	$413,086
54	$2,400	$378,304	$0	$463,593	$0	$444,113	$0	$446,133
55	$2,400	$411,160	$0	$500,681	$0	$479,642	$0	$481,823
56	$2,400	$446,645	$0	$540,735	$0	$518,013	$0	$520,369
57	$2,400	$484,969	$0	$583,994	$0	$559,454	$0	$561,999
58	$2,400	$526,358	$0	$630,713	$0	$604,210	$0	$606,959
59	$2,400	$571,059	$0	$681,170	$0	$652,547	$0	$655,515
60	$2,400	$619,336	$0	$735,664	$0	$704,751	$0	$707,957
61	$2,400	$671,474	$0	$794,517	$0	$761,131	$0	$764,593
62	$2,400	$727,784	$0	$858,079	$0	$822,021	$0	$825,761
63	$2,400	$788,599	$0	$926,725	$0	$887,783	$0	$891,821
64	$2,400	$854,279	$0	$1,000,863	$0	$958,806	$0	$963,167
65	$2,400	$925,213	$0	$1,080,932	$0	$1,035,510	$0	$1,040,220
Total Investment	$105,600		$55,200		$19,200		$14,400	
Investment Gain	$925,213		$1,080,932		$1,035,510		$1,040,220	
Investment Gain	876%		1958%		5393%		7224%	

The Rule of 72

It's difficult to explain compound interest and visualize its effect over time. This is where the Rule of 72 comes in. Essentially, this rule provides a much-simplified way of doing the mental math to approximate compound growth.

Here's how the Rule of 72 works: Divide 72 by the expected annual rate of return. The resulting number is essentially the number of years it will take for this investment to double. If you do the complicated math needed to predict the compound growth of a fund at a certain rate, you will get nearly the same result as using the rule of 72. In other words, if you're earning 7.2 percent, the Rule of 72 shows that your investment would double in about 10 years.

Here's a simple example. If you were to invest $100,000 and it earned 7.2 percent each year without adding another dollar of your own money, the account would grow as follows…

> In 10 years it becomes $200,000
> In 20 years it becomes $400,000
> In 30 years it becomes $800,000

This example illustrates a simple, yet profound investing principle. However, in real life, no market based investment will grow by 7.2 percent every year.

The higher the rate of growth, the faster an investment can double. The lower the rate of growth the longer it will take to double. Using the Rule of 72, the following is a list of interest rates and the length of time it would take for an investment to double at that rate.

- 3% doubles in 24 years
- 6% doubles in 12 years
- 9% doubles in 8 years
- 12% doubles in 6 years
- 15% doubles in 4.8 years

Now, it's time for a reality check. These figures are meant to illustrate a point, rather than offer specific guarantees. Sadly, there are no investments that offer a guaranteed 9, 12, or 15 percent rate of return year after year. Anyone who says otherwise is probably running a scam.

Investments in the broad market over the past 100+ years averaged around a 12 percent rate of return each year, but this statistic can be deceiving. To be more accurate, during some years, the market decreased by more than 30%, while other years it increased more than 40%. While investing in the markets involves risk and the possibility of loss, it's the risk of loss that makes it possible for the significant growth that many investors have enjoyed.

We have illustrated how $100,000 can turn into $800,000 after thirty years if the investment earns 7.2 percent per year. You may still be wondering how this could be true. You've likely heard that if something sounds too good to be true, it probably is. While compound interest may seem like magic, it's not. It's simply math.

Compound interest works because God created math, and math works in an orderly and predictable way. The secret to success, as we have discussed, is *consistent investing over time*. While success of the investment is not guaranteed, the more consistent the investor, and the more time the investment is allowed to grow, the greater the likelihood of success.

But isn't investing just like gambling?

The simple answer is "no." But *why*?

Sadly, too many people view gambling and purchasing lottery tickets as innocent fun that could lead to vast wealth. The lottery is not a reliable way to gain wealth, and studies show that many lottery winners spend most of their winnings within about twelve to eighteen months. Many report they would have been better off had they never won the lottery. Essentially, gambling and the lottery are get-rich-quick schemes, and those who seek easy wealth do not develop the discipline and wisdom it takes to grow it the hard way. They lack the wisdom to manage that wealth well.

Consider this: if the lottery was the best way to gain wealth, then why don't we see rich people driving their BMWs and Mercedes Benzes to gas stations to buy out their stock of lottery tickets? Most people who buy lottery tickets would be far better off to take that money and place it into a good, diversified investment, and leave it alone until retirement. We expect that the vast majority of people who do this will have much more to show for their money than those who simply buy lottery tickets.

Principles for Growing Wealth

Now that we've covered some of the basics of saving, and you understand how compound interest works, let's turn our attention to four principles for growing wealth. We have found in our decades of working with families that those who live by these principles are more likely to be successful in growing wealth than those who do not.

Principle 1: Live on Less Than You Earn

Living on less than you earn is one of the simplest and yet most profound rules for life. If your level of consumption is the entirety of your income, you will have no margin for the inevitable "bumps" in the road of life. Do you have a car repair bill, doctor's bill, or have you missed a week of work because of illness? If you aren't living on less than you earn, there's no way to handle these unexpected expenses, other than pulling out your credit card and paying the money back with interest. Doing so will increase your monthly expenses, which can result in a downward spiral of debt.

To live on less than you earn, you'll need to create a spending plan, or budget. You can find a sample of our spending plan in the Resources section of our website, provided at the end of the book. To create a budget, every month you'll list your income and basic expenses. Then, you can allocate the amounts you will give, save, spend, and so on. In addition to growing your wealth, living on less than you earn also allows you to be even more charitable and fund the Lord's work.

Principle 2: Maintain Reserves (An Emergency Fund)

Living on less than you earn allows you the margin to build up an emergency fund. Many financial experts agree that about three to six-months' worth of living expenses is the ideal amount for an emergency fund. While we agree with this in principle, we don't find it concrete or helpful. We have found Dave Ramsey's recommendation of a $1,000 starter emergency fund to be a wise place to begin. Once you get into your mid 30's through 50's, a goal of $8,000 to $10,000 might be more appropriate. Obviously, those with higher incomes or more uncertainty regarding their income and expenses would need to increase the amount of their emergency fund to reflect that reality.

Emergency funds are for use when unexpected bills come your way. Once you dip into your reserve account, seek to refill it as quickly as possible, because you don't know when you might receive your next surprise bill. Please note that Christmas *does not* represent an emergency—it comes on the same day every year, just like clockwork. Make sure these funds are reserved for true emergencies.

It would be wise to set up a savings account at a bank which offers a high interest rate on savings balances. To find these, type "high yield savings account" into an internet search engine. Make sure the account offers FDIC insurance, and that its interest rate isn't so far above similar accounts that it seems too good to be true.

Principle 3: Pay Off and Avoid Consumer Debt

Do you recall the earlier discussion about compound interest? Well, this principle that can be powerful for investors is very destructive when it comes to debt. The interest portion of your debt payments compounds in a way that can greatly slow down the process of becoming debt free.

Is debt in and of itself sinful? Our answer is that debt is generally neither good nor bad. The use of debt might be sinful if it is motivated by an unwillingness to wait for God's timing, the drive to keep up with the "Joneses", a desire to be seen by others as powerful or successful, wanting to feel better about yourself, or viewing possessions as the source of your identity and value, just to name a few. It's the motivation of the heart that determines whether debt is good or bad or righteous or sinful.

Furthermore, we need to consider the wisdom of using debt. Regardless of the condition of one's heart, certain types of loans are just bad. Consider the following three examples. First, payday loans often charge an exorbitant amount of interest (typically 400% annualized).[10] Second, borrowing 100% of the purchase price of your home increases the risk of a negative outcome if home prices drop. This also increases the monthly cost of your mortgage if you have to pay private mortgage insurance (PMI) premiums. Third, spending

---

[10] https://paydayloaninfo.org/how-payday-loans-work/

more than 50% of your take home pay on your mortgage jeopardizes your ability to build wealth and pay off debt.

Here are a few stewardship principles to consider prior to taking out a loan:

- Debt always mortgages the future to pay for the present.
- The borrower is a slave to the lender (**Proverbs 22:7**). You have to repay your debt, and if you don't, the lender may have legal means to take your assets or income. It doesn't matter to the lender if you lose your job—the payment must be made.
- Debt always results in an overall lower standard of living for your family because the new monthly payment will leave you with less discretionary income.
- Debt decisions must make economic sense. The economic return of debt must be greater than the economic cost of debt. In other words, never borrow to pay for depreciating assets (i.e., a car), or for lifestyle expenses (i.e., vacation).
- There needs to be a guaranteed way to repay the amounts borrowed. You can't just borrow the money hoping you will have enough to pay it off in the future, or hoping you get a raise to make the payments.
- Borrowing may deny God the opportunity to provide for your needs.
- If you are married, your spouse must be in full agreement before borrowing. Even when there is full agreement, debt brings additional stress into a marriage.
- Cosigning a loan will put you at unnecessary financial risk (**Prov. 11:15, 22:26**).

When it comes to paying off debt, we find that the debt snowball method is very effective. The debt snowball involves listing all debts except for your mortgage from smallest balance to largest balance due. You would pay the minimum payment on all but the smallest debt. You would allocate every available budgetary dollar on the smallest debt in an effort to pay it off quickly. Once that debt is paid off, you roll the money you are paying on it down to the next smallest debt. Keep this process up until you are debt free.

Some object to the emphasis on the lowest balance. Instead, they argue that by focusing on paying off the highest interest rate first, one can get out of debt more quickly and pay less interest. There may be times when prioritizing a high interest debt may be in order. However, these individuals fail to realize that getting out of debt—like getting into debt—is not primarily mathematical, it's psychological.

We don't "math" our way into debt, we allow our impulse spending to lead us into it. Each morning, when you get up and get ready for the day, you feel the emotional/psychological weight of your debt. It's like a dark cloud that casts a shadow everywhere you look. This is why focusing on quick wins by knocking out small debts can be more meaningful for those drowning in debt. Once consumer debt is taken care of, investing can begin.

Finally, the best way to avoid debt is to have margin in our lives. Margin means that we don't spend all our income. We keep some of our income as savings to help us weather large, unexpected bills or drops in income. When you live with margin in your life, stress levels go down and your cash cushion increases. Practice delayed gratification. Don't buy things on credit; instead, her save and prepare for the expense. Your future self will thank you.

Principle 4: Invest for Retirement

Once you have paid consumer debt, you would be wise to put 10% to 15% of your income towards retirement. If you are late to the retirement savings scene, you may want to increase the rate to make up for lost time.

There are many different types of accounts that are designed for retirement savings. Perhaps the best way for most people to get started is to contribute to their employer's retirement plan, if they offer one (for example, a 401(k), 403(b), Simple IRA, or TSP).

The first priority for retirement savings is to take advantage of an employer match. Many employers will match contributions up to a certain percentage. For example, the company that I/we run, The Life Financial Group, Inc., offers employees a 401(k). If they contribute 5%

of their income toward the plan, we'll match 4% of their income. Our team members would be wise to take advantage of every free dollar we offer.

The second priority is to invest in after-tax or Roth accounts. Today, many employers offer Roth 401(k)s, which allow employees to contribute funds to the account that have already been taxed. These funds are then able to grow tax free. If your employer does not offer a Roth 401(k), you may want to establish your own Roth IRA. This can be done by working with a financial advisor, if you have one, or by working through a large firm like Fidelity, Vanguard, or Charles Schwab, for example. Please note that our referencing these organizations is not a recommendation or endorsement of their services.

As you are able, seek to max out the contributions to after-tax accounts. Different types of accounts have different limits, and these limits frequently change over time, so be sure to check the current limits prior to making contributions. (IRA and Roth limits in 2025 are $7,000 per person and $8,000 for those 50 years old and up). There are also income limitations for contributing to certain types of accounts, like IRAs and Roth IRAs. If an investor earns a high level of income, it may limit his ability to contribute.

Finally, the last priority is to choose an investment allocation. Some people ask us which account will have better performance, a Roth IRA or a 401(k). This is the wrong question. These account types, Roth IRA and 401(k), are nothing more than labels. What drives performance is the individual investments used in the account. For example, a retirement fund could use a savings account. It would have no investment risk, but it also wouldn't experience much growth. On the other hand, if stock based mutual funds are used, the level of risk increases, but so does the potential return.

When setting up a retirement account, the choice of investments is very important. Your financial advisor can assist you in choosing an investment mix that is well suited to meet your objectives. If you don't work with an advisor, you may want to select a "retirement target date" fund offered through the investment plan or account.

Retirement target date funds list different years, such as 2030, 2035, 2040, and so on. These years correspond to a potential retirement date, and an investor would choose a date nearest to when they expect to retire. The underlying investments automatically become more conservative as the target date draws nearer. These funds are not perfect, and in many cases, we prefer that investors choose an investment mix that is customized for their goals and risk tolerance. However, if the investor doesn't have the ability or interest in doing this work, and/or can't work with an advisor, the target date fund is an acceptable option.

Disclosure: *"Exchange Traded Funds and Mutual funds, including Retirement Target Date funds are sold by prospectus. Investors should carefully consider the investment objectives, risks, charges and expenses of these type of funds. This and other important information is contained in the prospectus, which can be obtained from your financial adviser or plan sponsor and should be read carefully before investing."*

"But I can't afford to invest."

We are fully aware that more than a few of you who read this section may feel discouraged and hopeless because you have done all you can and still don't have enough to invest for the future. Know that you are not alone. Being a good steward doesn't require a vast income or large investment portfolio. God has called you to be faithful where you are. He has called you to trust Him with what you have.

That being said, you still should prayerfully seek to improve your situation. Seek out a mentor who can help you evaluate your options and encourage your trust in God. It would be wise to review your budget/spending habits with them. They may have perspectives that would help you see things in a different, more helpful way. Look for ways to improve your earnings potential through education and/or experience. Avoid "get-rich-quick" schemes.

The Bible teaches us that it is God who gives us the ability to earn a living and gain wealth (**Deuteronomy 8:18**). If, in His providence, He does not see fit to provide that to you, can you still trust Him?

Six Rules for Investing

Now that we've covered some of the principles for investing and building wealth, we'd like to share Six Rules for Investing that we've found to be very helpful. By following these rules, investors may be able to save themselves a lot of grief and sorrow.

1. **Don't Gamble With Your Investments**. Too many people treat the stock market and investing like a get-rich-quick scheme. They expect to make significant amounts of money by taking unwise risks. The good steward seeks to make wise investment choices that have a good opportunity of increasing in value over time. The good steward takes risks, but those risks aren't so high that if things go badly they will lose everything. It's possible to be a successful investor while maintaining moderate risk.

2. **Look at the Track Record.** While past performance does not guarantee future results, they are important considerations when choosing an investment. Where possible, try to assess the consistency of the management team. For instance, a particular investment that has grown by 8% for the past 10 years may have recently experienced turnover in their management team. This information might change your decision to use that investment. This is especially important with regard to mutual funds. Information about many different types of investments can be found at www.morningstar.com.

3. **Avoid "Sin Stocks"**. As a Christian investor, the good steward seeks to align his faith with his actions and investments. You can minimize and/or avoid investing in companies that profit from alcohol, tobacco, casinos, pornography, and abortion. Our firm, The Life Financial Group, Inc, has been offering Biblically Responsible Investment (BRI) portfolios to our clients for many years. We'll discuss BRI in more detail in the next chapter.

4. **Pay Attention to Investment Expenses.** All investments have expenses or costs, sometimes referred to as an "expense ratio." These costs can add up over time. The good steward is

aware of these fees and expenses and seeks to minimize them when possible. Additional costs to consider are an investment's surrender penalty and withdrawal fee. However, not all investments have these penalties or fees. They are common with annuities and other insurance products. Oftentimes, these products pay large commissions to the salesperson.

5. **Seek Independent Research**. Don't just blindly believe slick sales pitches. Before investing in a product or service that is new to you, do your research. Look at more than the company's marketing materials. Do a web search for the product name, and read product and customer reviews. If you think a product may be too good to be true, it would be wise to also search for the product name and the word "scam" to see what others have to say.

6. **Keep it simple**! Complexity does not make an investment better. Oftentimes, we find that increased complexity does not necessarily improve overall returns. If an investment or strategy is so complicated that it's difficult to wrap your mind around it, you should not invest. If you are married, make sure your spouse understands what's going on, too. This way, if the Lord calls you home first, your spouse will be able to continue.

The Secrets to Investing Success

The title of this section might be a bit misleading. There is no "magic strategy" that works for every investment in every situation. However, the following principles can help the good steward find success over time.

1. **Take advantage of market corrections.** People often ask us if they should stop adding to their investment accounts because they are "losing money". They feel that adding money to a fund that is decreasing in value is like throwing good money after bad. The good steward, however, recognizes that market declines are a great time to invest. If the investment is sound, an investor can purchase more shares at a lower price. It's like shopping when everything is on sale. Rather than being bad

times to invest, market downturns are perhaps some of the best times to invest.

2. **Don't try to time the markets.** Picking the tops and bottoms of the market is a fool's errand, but that doesn't stop people from trying. The problem with this is that the future is fundamentally unknown to all but God. There is no way to predict the direction of the markets over the short term. However, we know from history that given enough time, markets do tend to go up. The good steward continues to invest through all market cycles.

3. **Don't Trust your Emotions.** We often buy based on intellect when we see that an investment is performing well, but we then sell out of fear when it's not doing so well. On average, one year out of every four will yield negative market returns. When an investment has a negative return, don't panic. If you're consistent, you won't need to fear.

4. **Buy low and sell high.** We just said that market timing is a bad idea, but in general, selling an asset while its price is down is also a bad idea. Try not to sell assets at a loss if you can avoid it. On the other hand, if asset values are increasing, that might be a great time to take some of your profits to replenish cash holdings, or set funds aside for future purchases. Don't let fear or greed drive you to sell low and buy high.

Trust in God

It's important for you to guard your hearts against finding confidence and satisfaction in your wealth. Good stewards don't base their confidence in the future on their ability to earn a high income or on their investment prowess. They trust in God who richly provides them with all things to enjoy. There are no guarantees when it comes to money, but we can guarantee that God will provide, because He is faithful and keeps His Word.

Chapter 8:

Stewardship Principles for Managing Wealth

Now that we've addressed some of the basic information needed to grow wealth, we'll turn to the challenges of *managing* wealth. It doesn't take millions of dollars in a portfolio for someone to be concerned about how to manage their money. If the amount invested is significant to you, then this chapter is for you. Good stewards not only prepare for the future, but they also understand the resources entrusted to them must be cared for properly. In this chapter, we discuss several important stewardship principles related to setting goals, establishing a plan, and keeping a healthy mindset.

Guarding Your Heart While Investing

The good steward has many areas of concern and responsibility. There is potential tension between the need to care for the assets God has provided, while not becoming possessed by your possessions. You know Scripture commands you to carefully watch over your assets ("know well the condition of your flocks, and...herds" **Proverbs 27:23-27**), and elsewhere, it warns against the deceitfulness of riches ("but the cares of the world and the deceitfulness of riches and the desires for other things enter in and choke the word, and it proves unfruitful." **Mark 4:19**). So, how does the good steward guard against the negative effects of wealth? The following are several suggestions to help guard one's heart.

1. **Keep your walk with God close**—A close walk with God is cultivated through regular prayer and Scripture reading. As you read and meditate on the Bible, you are reminded of your place in this world. Here, you begin to understand that you deserve nothing, and all that you have comes from Him. As you pray, you are reminded of how dependent you are on God to accomplish anything.

2. *Be humble*—If you've experienced success, it's not because you are smarter or more spiritual than others. If God has blessed you with abundance and wealth, that blessing isn't about you… it's about a God who is pleased to bless the world through your life. You are not better than those who have less. Remember the message from **1 Peter 5:5:** *"Clothe yourselves with humility toward one another, for 'God opposes the proud but gives grace to the humble.'"*

3. **Give sacrificially**—We've said before that giving can help break the power of money in your lives. Gd stewards are generous with the income and assets God provides. You also look for opportunities to give beyond you comfort zone. You are willing to make sacrifices to support the ministries and causes that make a difference in this world. This helps you realize several things. First, you are not the ultimate owner of you belongings – God is. Second, you see you have power to effect good in this world by alleviating suffering and advancing the Gospel. Finally, you learn that you get more joy from generosity than from acquiring more toys.

4. **Serve in Addition to Giving**—In some ways, writing a check is easier than becoming personally involved in a ministry, but we believe being personally involved is just as important. When you do, you will find your heart more willing to pray for and give more to these causes. Roy had this experience when he spent time with a missionary who was serving at a radio station in the Caribbean. Getting involved by cutting down banana

trees and painting rooms helped move his heart toward the needs of others. By serving, you become even more grateful for what God has provided.

5. **Don't Flaunt Your Wealth**—It's not necessarily wrong to have nice things. It's okay to have expensive jewelry, fancy watches, and luxury cars, but be mindful of the condition of your heart if you purchase these items. Are you buying these things for your own enjoyment? Or do you own them to "show off" your wealth? Another factor to consider is that owning luxury items sometimes creates barriers to what you'd like to do for the Kingdom of God. It's unfortunate, but some people may have negative assumptions about you because of your wealth, and this can adversely impact your efforts in certain ministries. Each steward must determine in his own heart how God wants him to live. It is expected that sincere believers will come to different conclusions. Please be gracious with fellow stewards if their standard of living is different than yours.

Lord willing, these principles will help guard your heart from becoming cold toward others and the things of God. Now let's turn our attention to how the good steward manages God's assets.

Investing Goals

The good steward invests because the future is uncertain. How long will he or she be able to work? How long will retirement last? The good steward doesn't presume upon God's grace by ignoring the wisdom of Scripture, which calls us to prepare for the future. When investing, the good steward should consider the following goals:

Investing Goal #1: Growing Assets

Growth requires some amount of risk. Rather than just burying money in the backyard or leaving it in the bank to collect little interest, the good stewards seek to put their income to work. They'll invest their income in assets that have a good chance of increasing in value over time. These assets could include real estate, businesses, and/or investments like stocks, bonds, and mutual funds.

Investing Goal #2: Honoring Your Convictions

Socially Responsible Investing, also known as ESG (Environmental, Social, Governance) Investing, has increased in popularity. This view of investing realizes that investment dollars can have a real impact on our world. These types of investments seek to avoid companies which are considered to be harmful to the environmental and social order. While this sounds good in theory, in reality, the values behind ESG investing are often in opposition to a Biblical Worldview.

Biblically Responsible Investing (BRI) may be more appealing for the Christian investor, since BRI allows the good steward to invest God's wealth in a way that is consistent with Biblical ethics. With BRI, it is definitely possible to avoid investing in things such as tobacco, alcohol, casinos, pornography, and abortion. Biblically Responsible Investing is a way that Christians can live out their Christian testimony and convictions, even through their investing practices.

We understand that discussing these moral areas can be fraught with difficulty and disagreement. Choosing to invest in one company over another due to moral convictions is complicated. Some companies clearly promote a lifestyle that is in opposition to the Word of God (such as adult entertainment companies), while others may have a relatively small stake in products or services that are negative (like a grocery store that sells tobacco and alcohol products). Praise God that there are companies and products that wade through these thorny issues and can help Christians honor their convictions while managing and growing God's wealth.

Some investors want to know if investing in a Biblically responsible way will reduce the overall return potential. This is difficult to answer because, in part, past performance does not guarantee future results. That being said, we have found that investing in a BRI way does not necessarily mean that performance is enhanced or reduced. You may also want to be aware that the expenses for BRI and ESG funds tend to be slightly higher than their peers.

Investing Goal #3: Generating Income

The good steward eventually wants his assets to generate income that can be used to supplement his living expenses at some point in the future, such as retirement. We'll address the concept of sustainable withdrawal rates from investment portfolios later in the chapter.

Investing Goal #4: Managing Taxes

There are many ways that investing can impact an investor's taxes. On one hand, the use of tax-deferred retirement accounts can help reduce current income, thereby reducing the tax bill for the current year. On the other hand, focusing on tax-free accounts, such as the Roth IRA, may not reduce current year taxation but can reduce one's lifetime tax bill. Other factors, such as capital gains and dividends from non-retirement investments can cause an increased tax burden if not carefully managed. There are plenty of investment vehicles and/or investing strategies that can help limit ongoing taxation of non-retirement investment accounts.

Investing Goal #5: Managing Risk

There's no way to avoid risk in investing, or in life, for that matter. We must be willing to take *prudent* risks to properly manage our wealth. A prudent risk is one that takes individual factors into account: your goals, investment timeframes, risk tolerance, loss threshold, and ability to sit tight through a market downturn. Everyone has a different perception and tolerance for risk, which can make risk management a tricky aspect of investing.

One of the best ways to deal with market-based risk is through diversification. Mutual Funds and Exchange Traded Funds (ETFs) are investment options that invest in hundreds or thousands of different companies. Investors should avoid concentrating their wealth in just a few companies. ETFs may be a great option for those seeking the lowest cost investments or who want to avoid the taxation of capital gains distributions common in mutual funds. Mutual Funds may be great options for those seeking a professionally managed fund that doesn't simply try to replicate an index.

It's important to consider your risk tolerance and investment timeframe when choosing your mix of investments. If you don't work with a financial advisor, it may be helpful to choose either a risk-based model or a target date fund (this kind of fund increases its bond holdings each year it gets closer to the "target date"). A risk-based model consistently holds a certain risk level (i.e., Growth, Moderate, Conservative) while you hold the fund. It's important to keep in mind that as wonderful as diversification is, it cannot remove all risk from a portfolio.

Managing Emotions

One of the biggest risks in investing is also one of the most overlooked. Many investors may not be aware of this, but your emotions can cloud your judgment and lead you to make unwise choices.

To manage the emotional side of investing, you must first recognize the types of emotions that can influence your investment decisions. According to behavioral scientists, there is an *emotional cycle of investing* that reflects how investors feel during market highs and lows. We buy with optimism, which can escalate to a sense of euphoria if we hit the point of maximum financial risk. When the market declines, the emotions quickly become negative and travel on a downward slope, with positive emotions emerging once again when the market begins to perform well.

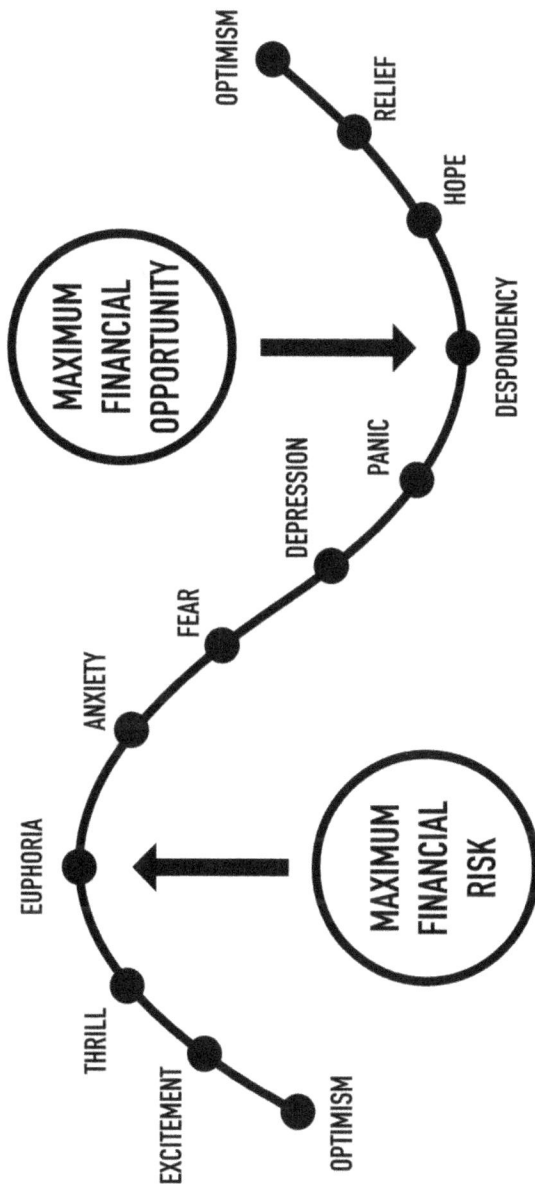

Cycle of Emotional Investing

Identifying Emotions

As you can see, there is a wide range of emotions when it comes to making investment decisions, but the two most influential ones that can derail a sound investment plan are fear and greed.

We can often reduce the potential for fear to impact our investment mix by choosing the correct risk level right at the outset. When investment markets and/or the economy are performing poorly, we can reduce our fear by tuning out the news and other media that contribute to this emotion. Additionally, frequently viewing our portfolios can cause us to make fear-based decisions. These rarely work out favorably for us as investors in the long-term.

Greed is subtle, easily overlooked, or called ambition, drive, work ethic, or even good stewardship. Ironically, it's fueled by the "fear of missing out", or FOMO. Back in the late '90s, some investments grew by +/-20% a year, while others (tech or internet-based funds) doubled year after year. Some investors felt that they were missing out on the great growth by settling for the comparatively small returns of non-tech funds. As investors became tired of not earning as much as their friends and co-workers, they abandoned higher-quality investments in favor of Dot Com funds. Unfortunately, these investors lost a significant amount of their principal when the tech bubble burst in the year 2000.

Dealing with Emotions

So, how do you deal with fear and greed? How do you deal with the emotional cycle of investing? How can you avoid it, and make sound investment decisions? As we explained in the last chapter, outsmarting the market isn't the secret to growing wealth. The secret is *remaining consistent over time*. While you are pursuing this goal of consistency, here are some practical ways to avoid making greed or fear-based decisions:

1. **Get the Facts**—Seek unbiased, third-party facts about your investment decisions. Don't get sucked into the hype and hysteria that's promoted on popular radio, TV shows, and commercials. These advertisements and discussions try to

instill fear so you will buy whatever they are selling. This is especially true during a market downturn.

2. **Seek wise counsel—Proverbs 11:14** says, *"In a multitude of counselors, there is wisdom."* Seek a godly person in your life who can help you sort through your options and make wise decisions.

3. **Sleep on your decisions**—Avoid knee-jerk reactions when investing. Slow down and take your time. Remember, God is in control and He will provide for all of your needs.

4. **Follow the Six Rules of Investing from Chapter Seven.**

Establish a Plan

Investing goals are helpful to guide you where you want to go, but *how* will you get there? By establishing a plan—a step-by-step process you will follow to achieve your goals. The following are suggestions for how to start.

Step 1: Assess Your Current Financial Condition

The first step in creating an investment plan is to assess your current financial condition. It's difficult to know where you want to go if you don't know your starting point

To begin, you'll want to create two important documents, both of which are essential to creating the foundation for a financial plan.

The first document is a budget. This can help you see how you spend your income right now, and whether or not your spending is in line with your long-term goals. Creating and working on a budget is difficult, but it's a helpful process and gives you a solid idea about the amount of money you have to work with.

The second document you'll want to create is a net worth statement. This document outlines every financial asset you own, as well as any outstanding debts. To calculate your net worth, subtract the total value of your debts from the total value of your assets. Your assets include the value of your home (if owned), bank accounts, and retirement accounts. Your debts include mortgages, home equity loans, car loans, credit card balances, student loans, and medical loans.

Obviously, this list of assets and debts is not meant to be exhaustive. If you have other assets or debts not listed in this section, you will include them, as well.

Step 2: Work with a Financial Professional

The good steward understands when it might be wise to bring in an expert who is able to help them better direct their thinking and craft a plan that helps them meet their objectives. We do acknowledge that not every person needs to work with an advisor. Some individuals understand the options, are well suited to wade through the markets, and can make the right choices, but many others are not well suited for investing on their own. The good steward understands their own skills, abilities, and temperament when it comes to financing and investing and makes decisions accordingly. Those who are not interested in such decisions can certainly outsource those responsibilities.

Even when a steward is comfortable managing his own finances, he may work with a trusted financial professional for the benefit of his spouse, especially when his spouse doesn't have the same interest or ability to manage investments. Also, if the spouse primarily responsible for financial decisions passes away first, the financial professional can continue to manage their investments and cash flow. This allows the surviving spouse the time needed to grieve without worrying about money.

Regardless of your choice of whether or not to work with a financial professional or manage your wealth on your own, it's important to share the entire financial picture with your spouse. Providing for your family is a crucial part of stewardship, even after the Lord has called you home. Share financial plans and information with your spouse at least once a year, even if they aren't interested. Roy and I both draft an annual financial update and share this document with our wives. Should we pass away before our spouses, they will at least know what resources are at their disposal.

How Financial Professionals Get Paid

There are essentially two different ways that those in the financial services industry get paid. First, they may earn a commission, which is paid for facilitating a transaction. This form of compensation should be anywhere from 1% to 7% or more, based on the specific products being sold. Second, the advisor may earn an annual advisory fee based on the amount of money under advisement. Fees are compensation for advice and investment management. Typically, annual advisory fees can be as high as 1.5% or as low as 0.3%, and are paid directly from the investment portfolio. In our experience, most financial advisors charge around 1% a year to manage money. When working with a financial professional it's also important to understand how he gets paid. If an advisor is uncomfortable discussing his compensation, it's likely he isn't working with your best interests in mind.

Five Things to Look For When Choosing an Advisor

Beyond understanding compensation, we have five additional recommendations when looking for a financial advisor:

1. **Find a believer who shares your convictions**. Since you're seeking advice on how to manage God's wealth, consider hiring a Christian advisor who prays with you and seeks Biblical wisdom.

2. **Understand the advisor's training and education.** Certifications for financial professionals can vary greatly. While designations and certificates don't guarantee that you're working with a great advisor, they can certainly indicate the advisor's commitment to learning and growing in their craft.

3. **Find someone with experience**. We recommend that you work with advisors with at least ten years of experience managing money. This is a long enough time period to see how they've weathered economic ups and downs. If you choose to work with an advisor who is new to the industry, make sure he works with mature advisors who can support him.

4. **Character matters: choose someone who follows his own advice.** Your financial advisor will learn a lot about you, so it's reasonable for you to ask about *him*. Request a copy of your advisor's credit report or credit score. A low score may be an indication that the advisor is a financial basket-case. To learn more about an advisor's history, you can also do a broker check

through the Financial Industry Regulatory Authority (FINRA) website.

5. **Find an advisor who practices holistic financial counseling.** There are several important dimensions to planning your financial future. The most important are: estate planning, tax planning, investment planning, insurance planning, and charitable planning. Without them, your plan will be incomplete. Make sure your advisor is prepared to help you harmonize these elements.

Professional Designations

There are many designations, but the two that we believe to be particularly important are the Certified Financial Planner™ (CFP®) and Certified Kingdom Advisor (CKA). An advisor with the CFP designation will have well-rounded knowledge and can address a variety of areas in financial planning. An advisor with the CKA designation understands the elements of financial planning from a Biblical perspective, and in that sense, can help you become an even better steward.

Step 3: Keep It Simple, Adjust As Needed

Occam's razor (14th Century philosopher William of Occam's "law of parsimony," or seeking explanations with the smallest number of parts or steps) suggests that the simplest solution is often the best solution. This is no less true in the world of financial planning. It's not necessary for you to have a one-hundred page document in your hands that explains your investment strategy. While large documents do have some value, they're rarely looked at due to their overwhelming size and complexity. In our opinion, it's better to have shorter, concise documents that outline where you are as well as the next steps you'll need to take to reach your desired goals.

Also, the more complicated the plan, the less likely you are to stick with it. A complicated plan is less likely to work because it will have so many moving parts. Some financial professionals' recommendations are so complicated that it's difficult to wrap your mind around them. Good stewards avoid implementing plans they don't understand. The best financial plans are comprehensive enough to address the critical dimensions of financial planning, yet simple enough to track progress made toward your goals.

It's important to keep in mind that a plan becomes outdated the moment it's written, because it makes assumptions about certain factors such as your income, cost of living, and market conditions. These factors will change over time, and they can differ from the initial plan projections. This means that you and your financial advisor will need to pay attention to your level of income, major life changes, and the performance of your investments to make adjustments as needed. Also, don't abandon your plan when the market is down. Consider it an opportunity to review and potentially adjust your plan.

Retirement Goals

The topic of retirement can feel overwhelming for many retirees. How can you know if you're ready to retire? What do you need to do to *stay* retired? In this section, we'll discuss five goals to consider in your retirement planning. This is not an exhaustive list of retirement goals, but it is a starting point from which you can develop your own.

Retirement Goal #1: Simplicity Over Complexity

When it comes to investing, many of us have a disjointed collection of accounts, assets, and advisors, which makes it difficult to plan for the future in a cohesive or systematic way. Many retirees have multiple retirement accounts, which can be difficult to track. Combining accounts can make it easier to manage finances in retirement.

Another way to simplify managing your accounts is to work with one advisor who can look at the big picture, rather than with multiple individuals who may not see or understand how their efforts are being duplicated. It's also possible for one advisor to contradict the strategies that another has already put into place. Finally, consider simplifying your financial picture. Do this with the "non-financial" spouse and those who may take care of your assets after you're mentally unable to manage yourself. You may understand and be able to handle all of the moving parts, but will your spouse or heir be able to do the same?

Retirement Goal #2: From Uncertainty to Certainty

One of the most challenging aspects of retirement planning for married couples is managing changes in income at the first death. This is a challenge because when the first death occurs, the smallest of the two Social Security benefits goes away. Likewise, pension income could disappear when the pensioner passes if the single life payout option was selected.

Here are a few suggestions to reduce the likelihood and severity of a loss in income at the first death:

1. Consider delaying Social Security for the spouse with the larger benefit until they reach full retirement age or later. When both spouses are receiving social security income they need to anticipate what will happen at the first death. When this happens, the smallest of the two social security payments goes away. Therefore, when the spouse with the largest benefit delays starting their social security income, they increase the amount of income the surviving spouse may receive.

2. Regarding pensions, select the income option that provides 75% to 100% joint and survivor benefits. This will allow the amount of income to remain the same after the first death.

3. While we don't love annuities, they may help by providing guaranteed income. Some annuities offer income riders that can provide a guaranteed income stream for the rest of your life (and potentially your spouse's). It is important to note that

144

guarantees are based on the claims-paying ability of the insurance company, not the US government.

These listed options may not be right for everyone, but they can certainly help create a stable stream of income.

Retirement Goal #3: Live Debt Free

Retirement is not a time to accrue debt; it's a time to eliminate and avoid it. The ideal is to be debt-free before you retire. Pay off all credit card bills, vehicles, and your mortgage as soon as possible. Understand that the more debt you carry into retirement, the greater your need will be for income.

Retirement Goal #4: Use a Sustainable Withdrawal Rate

A large factor in retirement planning is understanding how much you can sustainably withdraw from your retirement accounts without causing a significant risk of outliving your assets. The good news is, figuring out sustainable withdrawal rates isn't rocket science.

For example, if your accounts grow at a rate of 5 to 7% per year, and you're withdrawing 10 percent per year, obviously, you will run out of money at some point. Your account growth can't sustain the amount of your withdrawals.

A general rule of thumb we use with our clients is that they can withdraw about $1,000 per month for every $250,000 of invested assets. This represents a 4.8% withdrawal rate. The greater the rate of withdrawal, the greater the likelihood that income will be depleted from the account. The lower the rate of withdrawal, the less likely the account is to run out of money. Following this recommendation isn't a guarantee that you'll outlive your money, but a wise investor will consider reducing the rate of withdrawal when account performance falls below expectation.

Retirement Goal #5: Have an Emergency Reserve

One of the best ways to avoid debt is by establishing an emergency fund. This is especially true during retirement. We often find that retirees fall into one of two extreme categories: those without an adequate cash reserve, and those with far too large of one. However, for many retirees, $15,000 to $20,000 is plenty of money to handle the majority of emergencies. The larger one's budget is, the larger the emergency reserve should be.

Cash should be the only thing you hold in your emergency fund. We strongly suggest that you don't use home equity or credit cards for this fund. Consider using a high yield savings account instead. These typically offer a higher interest rate than most local banks, so you can earn while you save. They also offer FDIC insurance.

We suggest that you don't give into the temptation to invest your emergency reserves. This account is supposed to be simple and boring (i.e., it should not be up big one year and then down big the next year), and when an emergency does happen, you don't want to find that investment values have declined, leaving you with a much smaller emergency reserve.

In addition, if investment withdrawals are a part of your retirement income plan, it would be wise to keep 18 to 24 months' worth of income in cash within an investment account. We suggest doing this because if markets decline early in retirement and you're selling shares that are dropping in value, you'll burn through your money quickly. However, if you keep cash inside of an investment account, you can withdraw from the cash when markets are down, rather than selling mutual funds that are dropping in value to obtain the funds. This prolongs the lifespan of your account, and as markets recover, shares of your investment account can be sold to replenish the cash you withdrew.

Successful Redeployment

This may come as a surprise, but the Bible never discusses retirement. The only reference that even comes close to the modern-day concept is in Numbers 8:23-26, when the Levites are expected to step down from their duties at the age of fifty to help and serve the younger priests.

Even though the Bible doesn't discuss retirement, we recommend that retirees use their lifetime of experiences, knowledge, skills, abilities, and expertise to benefit others. Our golden years aren't meant for laziness or self-indulgence; we should serve the Kingdom by supporting various ministries and investing in our grandchildren. Thinking of retirement as "redeployment," can help you find or enhance your sense of purpose while helping others.

How to Manage Investment and Retirement Taxes

You may have heard the common phrase that nothing is certain in life except for death and taxes. While it's impossible to avoid death, there are things we can do to better manage our taxes in retirement. Most good tax preparers seek to reduce your current year tax bill as much as possible. This is often done through funding pre-tax retirement accounts such as a Traditional IRA or 401(k). Instead, we want to focus on reducing our *lifetime* tax bill. For example, it might make sense to intentionally pay a slightly higher tax bill in one year if you can receive potentially significant reductions or benefits in subsequent years.

The following are tips on how to reduce and manage taxes before and during retirement:

Tip #1: Focus on Tax-Free Investments Over Tax-Deferred

Investing in tax-free assets over tax-deferred can be a good strategy to help minimize your taxation in retirement. Roth IRAs and Roth 401(k)s allow you to receive "tax-free" income, assuming two requirements are met: you are at least age 59 ½, and have had a Roth account for at least five years. Contributions to these accounts have already been taxed, therefore the growth is entirely tax-free.

On the other hand, contributions to tax-deferred accounts such as traditional IRAs or 401(k)s can reduce your taxable income. While this may seem like a good idea, you may simply be kicking the proverbial "tax can" down the road. Eventually, when withdrawals begin, they will be fully taxed as ordinary income.

Tax-deferred accounts also have the potential to create a tax burden for your children in the future. For example, if you pass away and leave a $1 million IRA to your children, they will be forced to withdraw all of the money from the account within 10 years of your death. If your children are in a high tax bracket, these withdrawals could be taxed heavily. For this reason, wise investors seek to prioritize contributions to tax-free accounts during their working years.

Tip #2: Take Advantage of Roth Conversions

If you have a significant amount of money in tax-deferred accounts, such as Traditional IRAs or 401(k)s, it may be wise to convert a portion of that money to a Roth IRA. The amount converted will be taxed as ordinary income in the year of the conversion, but the future growth of those funds would be tax free. If you do choose to do a Roth conversion, the converted amount must remain in the new account for a minimum of five years. We strongly recommend that you consult with a tax professional to determine if a conversion is right for you, and if so, the right amount.

Tip #3: Taxation of Mutual Funds Versus ETFs

Mutual funds and exchange traded funds (ETFs) are simple investment vehicles which offer diversification and the opportunity for growth. However, ETFs differ from mutual funds in that they have a specific tax advantage.

When an investor holds mutual funds outside of a retirement account, they may have to deal with tax liabilities generated by those funds. By law, mutual funds are required to pay out dividends and capital gains in the form of taxable distributions, even if those distributions are reinvested. To add insult to injury, you may need to pay taxes on mutual fund distributions, even if the fund has lost value over the course of a year.

Being mindful of the potential tax implications of mutual funds, the good steward may decide to invest in exchange-traded funds (ETFs) instead. Unlike mutual funds, ETFs are not required to pay out capital gain distributions.

Tip #4: Don't Forget to Satisfy Your RMD

As of the publication of this book (2024), once you reach the age of 73 ½, the government requires you to withdraw a minimum amount of money out of your retirement accounts with the exception of Roth accounts. These withdrawals are known as Required Minimum Distributions, or RMDs. The distributions are fully taxable as ordinary income, which means that large IRAs generate large RMDs, and could have negative tax implications. It's also important to withdraw your RMDs on time, because if you don't, the IRS will impose a 25% penalty tax for late or missed RMDs.

RMDs are yet another reason why someone would choose to invest in or convert to a Roth IRA, since Roths do not impose RMDs, and any withdrawals taken from Roth accounts (after age 59 ½ at the time of writing) are not taxable. Legislation changes often, so we encourage you to talk to a financial professional or check your latest legislation to make sure you are following the latest guidelines and rules set in place.

Tip #5: Consider Qualified Charitable Distributions (QCDs)

If you are of RMD age (currently age 73 ½) but don't want to deal with the tax consequences, you may want to consider Qualified Charitable Distributions (QCDs). Rather than taking your RMD in cash, you could designate a qualified non-profit organization to receive your distribution. This allows you to avoid paying taxes on up to $100,000 of IRA distributions each year while funding your church or favorite ministry(ies).

It's possible to satisfy the distribution requirement by doing a partial RMD with the rest as a QCD. This is known as a partial QCD. It allows you to receive some income while eliminating part of the tax burden.

With QCDs, your investment company will send a tax reporting form, indicating that you received taxable income. However, since a QCD is not taxable, be sure to show your tax professional the donation receipt.

Tip #6: Donate Highly Appreciated Assets

Another way investors can manage their taxes is to donate assets that have significantly grown in value (a highly appreciated asset). This could be a stock, mutual fund, real estate, and/or even business interests. Note, there are many rules that govern valuing assets such as real estate or businesses so be sure to work with a tax and valuation professional before you donate.

For example, if you purchased a stock worth $10 and it eventually grew to $100, you would realize a gain of $90. That gain would most likely be taxable. If, however, you chose to donate that share worth $100 to a non-profit organization (like your church), you would potentially be able to deduct the gift as an itemized deduction, while avoiding capital gains tax at the same time. There are limits to how much you can contribute based on your level of income, and these limits can change from year to year. For this reason, consult a tax and/or financial professional prior to donating appreciated assets.

Finally, a word of caution: you should never donate an asset that has lost value. For example, consider the purchase of a stock for $50 a share that is now only worth $20. If you choose to donate that stock, you're only able to deduct the value of the shares on the date you make the gift. You'll get no credit for experiencing a loss of $30. If, however, you choose to sell the share at $20 and then donate the cash, you can claim the $30 loss on your tax return (to help offset other gains), and deduct the $20 donation on your tax return (Schedule A).

Tip #7: Donor Advised Funds (DAF)

Donor Advised Funds (DAF) are accounts you establish at a charitable foundation. Cash or highly appreciated assets are donated to the DAF, which provides a tax deductible receipt. As the donor, you have the right to advise the foundation on how the contributed funds are to be dispersed among other non-profit organizations. You can recommend which organizations to support, how much support they will receive, and the frequency and timing of when they will get the funds. The organizations must be 501©3 and approved by the foundation. Funds retained in the DAF can be invested. This allows time for you, the donor advisor of the fund, to decide which organizations will receive your gifts.

Donors have many choices—both secular and Christian—when choosing which organization to establish as their DAF. It would be wise to consider whether the foundation shares your values and beliefs. Some secular foundations have recently refused to donate to certain Christian ministries according to their closely held religious beliefs, alleging discrimination or intolerance. Therefore, if you set up a DAF through a Christian sponsor organization, they are more willing to administer the fund according to your Christian convictions.

While you can give from a DAF after your death, that's not its primary purpose. The primary purpose of a Donor Advised Fund is to get a current year tax deduction while spreading your giving out over several calendar years. For example, if you sell a business or property that results in a large tax bill, donating to charity would allow you to spend less on taxes.

Donor Advised Funds can also encourage the next generation in their giving. For instance, my parents, Roy and Lana, are leaving half of their estate to charity by giving it directly to a DAF. They have listed the four Russell children as successor donor advisors, which means that after their deaths, we will have the joy of choosing which ministries to bless in the memory of our parents.

Two Donor Advised Funds commonly used by Believers are the National Christian Foundation (www.NCF.org) and the Waterstone Foundation (www.Waterstone.org).

Do You Need Help?

As you can see, there are many factors to keep in mind when managing your assets through retirement. If you feel that you need help, consider signing up for a free stewardship review with The Life Financial Group, Inc. visit www.thelifegroup.org/meeting.

In the next chapter, we'll discuss the stewardship implications of transferring God's wealth to the next generation.

PART 3 - The Good Steward's Impact

Chapter 9:

Transferring Wealth: The Good Steward's Guide to Estate Planning

The question, "How much is enough?" doesn't just apply to how extravagant one's lifestyle is, or how much they have saved for retirement. We also want to ask this question when considering how much we may leave behind for our children or heirs. It's estimated that the Baby Boomer generation (born between 1945-1960) controls more than $70 trillion of America's wealth.[11] This means that over the next thirty years, more wealth will be changing hands than at any other point in human history.

This is why asking, "How much is enough?" matters when considering how to handle your estate. Is the next generation prepared to steward the wealth that the Lord has entrusted to you? Will leaving them a significant inheritance help or hinder their walk with God? Will that money reduce their drive to grow and manage their finances well? How much of what the Lord has entrusted to you will be used for Kingdom purposes? These questions are important because they help

---

[11] https://www.marketingcharts.com/demographics-and-audiences/household-income-225380

us begin to understand just how important estate planning is for Christian stewardship.

Elements of Estate Planning: Essential Questions

An estate is comprised of all of your assets: financial (businesses, bank accounts, investments), physical (house, car, belongings), and even digital (social media accounts, email accounts, files stored in the cloud). A time will come when you are no longer able to care for these items yourself, and as a Good Steward, you need to develop an estate plan for their continued care. There are many things to consider when creating an estate plan, and in this chapter, we'll address the following essential estate planning questions:

- What is an estate plan and who needs one?
- What documents are included in an estate plan?
- What makes an estate plan uniquely Christian? What's in a Christian will?
- What is probate, and how can I avoid it?
- What are the best ways to give to charity at my death?

Essential Question #1: What is an estate plan, and who needs one?

An estate plan is a set of documents that outline what you'd like to happen with your belongings both while you're alive and after your death. This can include your home, cars, valuable collections, bank accounts, investments, and other assets. In addition to what you'd like to happen with your belongings, these documents also indicate the individual(s) you want to care for any minor children in the event of your death. It would be wise for those aged eighteen and older to have an estate plan.

Essential Question #2: What documents are included in an Estate Plan?

An estate plan is a set of documents including a will, financial power of attorney, medical power of attorney (which may include an advance directive or living will), and a living trust, which is optional.

Your last will and testament, or will, is a document that expresses your wishes regarding what happens to your possessions after you die. Typically, you'll leave all your estate to your spouse when you die. If your spouse has already passed away, then you'll divide your assets among any children and/or grandchildren. Your will also names the person responsible for making sure your wishes are honored, also known as an executor or executrix. It also names the Trustee, the person who will handle your money for any children who aren't old enough to handle the funds on their own. A will also appoints a guardian, the person who will take care of any children under the age of eighteen following your death.

Power of attorney (POA) documents are another extremely important part of an estate plan. Your will addresses what happens after your death, and the POA addresses what happens while you are still living. At the moment of your death, the POA loses its authority, and the will comes into play.

Each person needs to have two different types of POAs: financial and medical. The financial POA authorizes someone to represent your financial and/or legal interests when you are unable to do so yourself. They can open and close accounts, take out loans, and much more. These powers can be durable or springing. Durable POAs are in full force the moment they are signed. There is nothing else that needs to happen before these powers can be used. Springing POAs are only in full force once a certain condition is met, such as mental incompetence or incapacity. Often, these powers require the written opinions of several medical professionals before the document springs into action. For this reason, we encourage durable POAs.

The second type of Power of Attorney is the medical POA. It authorizes someone to make medical decisions on your behalf if you are unable to do so yourself. This document may also include your choices as to what kind of medical care you would or would not like or you could keep this information in a separate document called a living will.

A living will is a document that informs your medical providers what your choices are regarding medical treatments to keep you alive.

This comes into play when your death is imminent and/or you are unable to communicate your desires otherwise. This document can include a "Do not Resuscitate" (DNR) instruction which prohibits resuscitation. A living will specifies whether or not you want life-supporting treatments or procedures. Whereas the living will only informs, the Medical POA authorizes someone to act. Be aware that this person can override the living will should the facts of your condition and the available treatments warrant it.

The final document that is sometimes included in an estate plan is a living trust. We say "sometimes" because the majority of people probably don't need it. A living trust is a document designed to avoid probate and provide ongoing management of your assets. *Probate* is the court-overseen process that makes sure your belongings and assets are distributed properly, per your wishes. We find that those who live in states with cumbersome probate systems and/or have complicated estates benefit most from establishing and funding a living trust. (Probate will be further discussed and explained in **Essential Question #4.**)

Think of a living trust as a container that holds your assets. You can transfer your home, bank accounts, and non-retirement investments into the trust. Once you do so, the trust owns these assets. This means that when you die, probate will be avoided for assets that are held in the trust. A living trust acts like a will in some respects, because it specifies how funds will be distributed after your death. However, just having a living trust doesn't necessarily mean your heirs will avoid probate—you have to go through the process of retitling your assets so the trust is the owner. One additional document that comes along with the trust is something called a "Pour-over-will." This will catches any assets that you may have forgotten to place into the trust, takes them through probate, and then places the assets into the trust.

Choosing an Executor and Power of Attorney

Some of our clients struggle to choose an executor or POA. Many individuals choose to list all of their children as co-executors and/or co-POAs. They may do this to avoid the appearance of playing favorites, or to prevent conflict among their children. In our experience, appointing co-executors or POAs can create more frustration and conflict for your heirs. We recommend that you list one person as the primary executor or POA, then list a backup and additional backups as needed.

How do you choose an executor or personal representative? We recommend considering at least three factors when making your decision. We call these factors the "Three C's": character, competence, and convenience. You should assess these C's in this particular order when making your selection.

- **Character**: Does the person have and display a moral character that is in line with your values? For example, you wouldn't choose an alcoholic or drug-using family member.

- **Competence:** Is the person capable of making rational decisions and carrying out the wishes you have written in your estate planning documents? Competence doesn't mean they know all the answers, but that they know when to enlist the services of others who can help guide them. They know how to ask lawyers, financial advisors, and/or doctors the right questions to determine what is truly best for you.

- **Convenience**: Which child or family member lives closest to you? If you have one child who lives a few miles away versus another child who lives across the country, logically, you'd appoint the child who lives closest to you, provided they have character and competence.

The Problem with Do-it-Yourself Estate

We strongly recommend that you work with an attorney to create your estate plan, preferably one who shares your values and convictions. If you do it yourself or find a shortcut online, you could unintentionally make decisions that aren't in the best interests of your family or your heirs.

We've had clients bring us estate planning documents that were prepared through a free online estate planning website. The problem with these do-it-yourself online estate planning tools is that when you don't understand the concepts or terms being used, you can cause significant harm to your family. In one case, a client listed his brother as executor of his estate and power of attorney, instead of his wife. By making his brother the executor, he was cutting his wife out of financial decisions for the estate. By making him POA, he was also excluding his wife from making financial and medical decisions on his behalf. It would have made much more sense if this client had listed his brother and an additional person as backups, and listed his wife as the primary.

Since you don't know what you don't know, it is wiser to work with someone who can guide you in the estate planning process. We understand that hiring an attorney can be costly, but the cost of making unintentional mistakes could be much higher.

Planning

Essential Question #3: What makes an Estate Plan uniquely Christian?

A Christian estate plan is one that is customized to reflect your Christian values and convictions. We encourage the use of a Christian will, which includes a preamble with your testimony of faith, and a challenge to your heirs to wisely manage what you are entrusting to them. You might start out with something like this, *"For me, to live is Christ, to die is gain. To be absent from the body is to be present with the Lord. Know that if you are reading this, I am with my Lord and Savior, Jesus Christ, who has fully paid for all my sins with His precious blood, and has set me free from the tyranny of the devil..."* **(Philippians 1:21)** You may want to go on to share some of your personal testimony. What has Christ done for you? How has he changed your life? Remember, this is your last chance to speak into the lives of your loved ones. Encourage them to keep short accounts with God.

The following four questions are not meant to be exhaustive, but may help you consider how to customize your Will according to your values and convictions.

1. **Have you considered leaving some of your estate to ministry at your death?** Many Christians consider this their final act of stewardship, but a word of caution may be due at this point. A wise thought leader in Christian Financial Stewardship, Ron Blue, is fond of saying, "Do your giving while you're living so that you're knowing where it's going." While there's nothing inherently wrong with charitable giving at death, it shouldn't be the only form of giving.

   We strongly encourage Good Stewards to give sacrificially throughout their lives and give generously at death. Stewards miss a great blessing when they delay giving until death, when they will have no more need for their money. While giving at death may be generous, it's not sacrificial. (See **Essential Question #5** for additional ideas on the best ways to fund ministry and reduce taxation through your estate plan.)

2. **At what ages should your children gain control of the assets in your estate?** Children age eighteen and older are given control of the assets left to them in an estate, unless there are restrictions in the will. In our experience, it is not wise to leave a large estate to an eighteen-year-old with no restrictions or guidance.

   We don't know about you, but we probably wouldn't have made the wisest decisions with those funds when we were eighteen! Instead of leaving young heirs a lump sum, consider giving them one-third of the money at age twenty-one (this will allow them to get their "stupid" out without wasting all of the funds), another third at age twenty-five, and the remainder at age thirty. This is just one of many ways to encourage wisdom and reduce the chances of funds causing harm, when the intent is for them to be helpful.

3. **Is a Christian education a priority for you?** If it is, your will may state that the trustee is authorized to pay for your children's K-12, college, and post-graduate Christian educational pursuits. If you desire to provide for these educational expenses, make sure there is enough money to cover them, either through assets in the estate, or life insurance.

4. **Who will raise your children in the ways of the Lord?** We find that this is one of the hardest choices young parents have to make. Your choice doesn't need to be perfect—it just needs to be *your choice*. You can start by considering family members. If none of them would be appropriate, consider close family friends, and/or others at church who would be able to assist with this need. The idea is to ask someone who knows your family and supports your values and parenting style. It's always a good idea to ask them if they are willing to perform this function before just volunteering them in your will.

Essential Question #4: What is probate, and how can I avoid it?

As addressed in Essential Question #2, probate is the court-overseen process of ensuring your assets are distributed to your heirs, charities, and other beneficiaries according to your wishes. The word "probate" can have a negative connotation, but really, it's not necessarily a bad thing. Probate can cause some time delays and involve additional costs, but each state determines how easy or complicated the process will be. Some states, like California, make probate excessively complicated, time-consuming, and expensive. Other states offer a more streamlined approach. You will want to discuss your state's probate rules with an attorney or estate planning expert.

Let's take a look at the advantages and disadvantages of probate.

Advantages of Probate:

- Probate guarantees the orderly transfer of assets, and it's done publicly, under the supervision of the court.

- It provides valid title transfer of assets, ensuring it is done legally.
- It settles all beneficiary disputes of estate distributions in court.
- Creditor claims against your estate can only be made for a limited time, as directed by the laws of your state.
- If you have more debts than assets, probate ensures that your assets are used to cover as many debts as possible. Any remaining unpaid debts are canceled, preventing creditors from going after your heirs.

Disadvantages of Probate:

- Probate can be expensive. The costs vary in each state, with the largest expense coming from legal fees. A lawyer may charge your heirs a flat rate, hourly rate, or 3 to 5% of the value of your estate for their services.
- Probate generally takes nine to twelve months. The amount of time varies by state, but probate can take even longer if your estate is complex.
- Court proceedings are inherently inflexible. The timeline is quite rigid when it comes to filing the correct documents, and your heirs must abide by the rules of your state.
- When your estate goes through probate, your will becomes public record. Your wishes for your estate, and your family matters are available for others to see. If you're a celebrity, public figure, or particularly private person, you may not want this information to be revealed. Also, certain people may look at the details of your will and try to take advantage of an heir to whom you left a generous amount of money.
- If you own property in more than one state, your executor or executrix will have to deal with *ancillary probate* (probate in multiple states). They will need to hire an attorney for each state in which you own real estate.

If you don't find this list of disadvantages appealing, you may want to consider the following methods to help avoid probate.

Avoiding Probate

There are three basic ways to pass assets to your beneficiaries (i.e., your loved ones) without involving probate.

The first way to avoid probate is with a funded living trust. "Funded" means that the ownership of your assets has been transferred to the living trust. Trusts are not assets, they're legal entities. Therefore, assets in a living trust avoid probate. When you pass away, only the assets that you own outside of the trust go through probate. The trust document would then instruct the successor trustees (typically your children) on how and under what conditions distributions are to be made to the beneficiaries. These trusts can easily cost more than $3,000 to set up. They are great if you own real estate in several states thus avoiding ancillary probate. In states where probate is much worse than others (i.e., California), we often recommend using the living trust. Due to the cost and complexity of living trusts, we generally try to avoid their use unless absolutely necessary.

The second method to avoid probate is to name beneficiaries on various types of accounts. For example, life insurance, annuities, and retirement accounts such as IRAs, Roth IRAs, 401ks (and more) allow you to name beneficiaries. At your death, the funds are transferred to your beneficiaries without going through probate.

Finally, titling your accounts correctly can also help avoid probate. The simplest way to do this is to use a "joint tenancy with rights of survivorship" (JTWROS) rather than having the account in your name alone. When one of the owners of the joint account passes away, the surviving owner automatically owns the account. Another way to title your assets to avoid probate would be to use "payable on death" (POD) or "in trust for" (ITF) for bank accounts. This allows you to designate beneficiaries on your bank savings, money markets, and certificate of deposits. Lastly, the use of "transfer on death" (TOD) can be used to name beneficiaries on non-retirement investment accounts. These designations bypass the Will, and also bypass probate. By using these creative titles, you can gain some of the same benefits of a living trust without the expense of creating one.

One question we often hear is, "Is it wise to add my child(ren) as joint owners on my home?" We generally discourage this, as it may create several unintended consequences, including but not limited to increased capital gains taxes for your children at your death, liability risk should your child be sued, and legal complications should your child go through a divorce.

Trust Mills

We have to warn you, that there are attorneys who may pressure you into establishing a trust you may not need. These people run "trust mills," where they host dinners and tell people about how terrible and expensive probate can be, even if they live in a state where probate isn't particularly problematic. Their proposed solution to avoid probate is to establish a trust, and they may ask you to spend thousands of dollars to set one up. If you buy what they are selling, you could end up spending more money on the trust than your heirs would spend in probate.

Essential Question #5: What are the best ways to give to charity after my death?

In our experience, we've seen Christians who give generously throughout their lives choose to continue their generosity at their death. There are at least four ways to give to charity after your death.

The first and easiest way to give to charity after your death is to **designate a charity as a beneficiary in your will**, and stipulate the amount or percentage to be given. The executor of your estate then writes a check to the charity from the estate's checking account. The money in the estate checking account comes from bank accounts, equity in your home, and other assets that are tax-free to your heirs. However, designating a charity as a beneficiary in your will may not be the most tax-effective way to give money to the ministry.

The second option for leaving money to charity is to **include the charity as a beneficiary of your retirement accounts**. Consider giving out of your IRAs, 401(k)s, and annuities, as these assets would be taxable to your heirs, but tax-free to non-profit organizations. This strategy reduces the amount your heirs would have to pay in taxes by giving out of taxable assets, and leaving the tax-free assets for them. This allows you to change your mind and update your beneficiaries free of charge. Otherwise, if you had listed the charity in your Will and later changed your mind, you'd have to pay an attorney to update your will.

If you're married, we recommend that you list your spouse as the primary beneficiary on your retirement accounts. When you do this, you are given the option of listing contingent beneficiaries. You would then list charities and/or your children as beneficiaries if your spouse predeceases you.

Third, you can leave money to charity by **establishing a Charitable Remainder Trust**. This type of trust provides a current year tax deduction, while also supplying an income during your lifetime. At your death, the remnant of the trust is paid to pre-selected charities. There are costs involved in establishing this kind of trust, as well as ongoing costs for preparing the trust tax return each year. For this strategy to be effective, the tax and/or income benefits must outweigh the costs.

We have clients who have used Charitable Remainder Trusts when selling farmland, real estate, and/or businesses. For instance, if you purchased land for $5,000 per acre decades ago, and today someone offers to buy your land for $100,000 per acre, you would realize a $95,000 capital gain. By placing the gains in a charitable remainder trust, you can write off the $100,000. This scenario is intentionally oversimplified for the sake of illustration. There are several factors which could increase or decrease the actual gain. Be sure to consult a tax advisor prior to acting upon this information.

The fourth way to leave money to charity is **through a Donor Advised Fund (DAF),** which we discussed in the previous chapter. You can designate a DAF as a beneficiary in your Will or retirement accounts. This can be helpful when you have many charities that you support, and/or you would like to involve your children in the gifting of these funds.

Estate Planning Applications

The information we've just covered is not exhaustive. We hope you've been able to get a sense of what is involved in estate planning, and that you've identified some of the potential pitfalls to avoid. Having a complete, well-thought-out estate plan is one of the best ways to show your loved ones how much you care about them. Please take action.

Here are a few application questions to consider:

1. **Do you have a will and power-of-attorney documents?** If you don't have these documents, we strongly encourage everyone to at least get them in place. It is wise to work with an attorney who can help you have documents that allow for the latest enhancements in the world of estate panning. Remember to include your testimony of faith in Jesus Christ in your will.

2. **Are your estate planning documents up to date?** If you have estate planning documents in place, it is important to periodically review them. Brush off the dust and take a look at what your documents say. Have you had a falling out with those in key roles within your estate plan? Are there children that can now fulfill those key roles? Do these documents reflect your current desires?

3. **Do your heirs know what to do when you die?** Hold a family meeting to discuss your plans. This is really helpful as we move through retirement. Do your children know what they need to know to honor your wishes (i.e., end of life situations or charitable intentions)? Do they know where to find your current estate planning documents? Do they know where your money is held (banks, investments, physical cash, or coins)?

As you consider these questions and their application to your life, remember to pray for wisdom and guidance so that you can leave an organized plan that demonstrates your love for God and your care for your loved ones after you pass away.

Chapter 10:

Hearing "Well Done"

As we wrap up this book, we want to address its title, *The Good Steward*. Essentially, we've suggested that as you read this book and apply the principles to your life, you can become a *Good Steward*. The goal of every Christian should be to hear the words, "Well done, my good and faithful servant" when we reach heaven.

However, being a good steward does not necessarily make one a good Christian. You can make all the right moves with money, and still fail in a thousand other areas of your walk with God and with others. We don't want to pretend that all God requires of the believer is to be good with money. And yet, in many ways, how we view and handle money can reveal much about our overall spiritual health and vitality.

In this conclusion, we want to address the dangers and rewards of good stewardship. We will then close this book by discussing stewardship as a process, not an event.

The Three Dangers of Good Stewardship

There are three big dangers that good stewards may face: pride, entitlement, and self-confidence. Let's examine each one.

Pride

Pride can manifest itself as a smug or haughty attitude. This can happen with good stewards who believe they are better than others who appear to be far less concerned with how they spend their money. They give 12 percent of their income to the church, save 15 percent for retirement, live within their means, help the poor, and spend next to nothing on themselves.

Consider **Jeremiah 9:23–24**:

> *Thus says the Lord: "Let not the wise man boast in his wisdom, let not the mighty man boast in his might, let not the rich man boast in his riches, but let him who boasts boast in this, that he understands and knows me, that I am the Lord who practices steadfast love, justice, and righteousness in the earth. For in these things I delight, declares the Lord."*

Good stewards can be tempted to boast about how good they are. You may have read all the way through this book and feel confident that you already do much of what we encourage. It's fine to be confident, but don't let your heart become proud in your stewardship. Rather, boast about your relationship with your Heavenly Father who richly provides you with all things to enjoy.

Entitlement

The good steward can also be tempted to feel that God owes them something because of how good they've been with their money. They may feel that God owes them riches, happiness, an easy life, good health, and more.

The feeling may not even be a conscious one; it may be rooted deep inside the heart. If this belief is subconscious, how can you become aware of it? Consider the following questions: When things aren't going your way, do you begin to feel like God hasn't held up His end of the bargain? Do you question your relationship with God if you don't get what you ask for? When things are going well, are you filled with gratitude towards God, or do you feel that you've earned your success?

Consider the Parable of the Prodigal Son (**Luke 15:11-32**). In this story, the younger brother demands his inheritance early. When he receives it, he leaves home and wastes the money on wild living. Later, he comes to his senses and returns to his father, who embraces him with open arms. The older brother, however, never leaves the father, never lives in a wild manner, and never does anything against the father. But we see how entitlement rears its ugly head when the older brother says to his father, "Look, these many years I have served you, and I never disobeyed your command, <u>yet you never gave me a young goat, that I might celebrate with my friends</u>." (**Luke 15:29**)

The older brother stayed with the father, and because of that, he believed that the father owed him something for his obedience. Those of us who strive to be good stewards may be more like the older brother than perhaps we'd like to admit. We may love the reward of good stewardship more than we love God himself.[12] Good Stewards can pursue all the right things for the wrong reasons. In this way, we can miss the whole point of stewardship, which is to bring glory to God by showing the world (and yourself) that He is more valuable to us than money and what it provides.

Self-Confidence

The final danger of good stewardship is self-confidence. When you live on less than you earn, save for the future, and invest for retirement, your assets tend to grow. As your assets grow, your confidence in the future is more closely tied to the amount of resources at your disposal.

Self-confidence starts off subtly at first. When an emergency comes up, you don't panic (which is a good thing), but you also don't pray (this is a bad thing). Rather, you use your emergency reserves to meet the expense.

Over time, you stop asking God for your "daily bread" because your pantry is full. You have enough money in your bank accounts and investment portfolios to meet all of your earthly needs. You don't pray for God's provision because you don't feel that you need Him.

Ultimately, your sense of security and peace becomes tied to your possessions, investments, and savings. When your investments are doing well, you feel great and believe you can face any challenge. But when they do poorly, you start to wonder if your

---

[12] To go deeper into this parable, we recommend Tim Keller's book, *The Prodigal God*.

ideas for the future will come to pass. If this happens, it clearly indicates that your sense of security is too closely tied to your savings.

So, what should you do about these dangers of good stewardship? Forget about working to become a good steward. No! The good steward acknowledges these dangers and seeks Christ's help to battle the love of money at the heart level. You can also go back and reread Chapter 6 for Paul's prescriptions on how to keep yourself free from the love of money.

The Ultimate Rewards for Stewardship

We not only believe that good stewardship is commanded in Scripture, but it also is also richly rewarded. We addressed the dangers of good stewardship in the last section because there is often a tangible, material blessing for wise stewardship. The book of Proverbs often indicates that when we save, work hard, give to others, and spend carefully, material blessings follow. But Scripture is also clear that this is not always the case, nor should we expect that God is obligated to provide material or financial blessings for our obedience.

There are ultimate rewards we can and should expect from God for our good stewardship. Let's take a look at two of these intangible, eternal rewards.

Hearing "Well Done"

If you recall in the Parable of the Talents, the master says to the first two servants who wisely managed the funds entrusted to them, *"Well done, my good and faithful servant. Enter into the joy of your master"* (**Matthew 25:21, 23**). These are the words every good steward longs to hear from the Lord.

To hear the words, "Well done, my good and faithful servant" means we've made God the highest priority in our lives. We chose Him over money and possessions. We made our stewardship decisions from a place of faith, rather than fear or greed, and we trusted God with the outcome.

Consider the word "joy" in this passage. The word joy can be taken in two different ways. On one hand, when we are a good steward with the resources entrusted to us, we bring joy to God. We enter into the joy of the father. We serve a joyful God who delights in His children. The second sense in which the word "joy" can be understood is the joy that we experience as we please the Father. We are filled with joy because of the Father's love and delight in us. When God becomes our chief treasure, we experience more joy—both in this life and in the life to come.

Treasures in Heaven

In **Matthew 6:19-24**, we are commanded to lay up for ourselves treasures in heaven. This happens when we value God more than money, as evidenced by our generosity toward others and toward the Church. Randy Alcorn wisely says that we can't take it with us, but we can send it ahead. Nothing done for God is wasted.

Even if you were the best investor of all time and earned 1,000% year after year, your return on investment could never be better than the return from the resources laid up in heaven. The math of kingdom generosity makes investing on this side of eternity seem boring. Don't get us wrong, you still should save and invest for your future here on earth. But those investments should pale in comparison with the value you place on investing in God's Kingdom.

Stewardship Is a Process, Not an Event

In one sense, good stewardship is simple: live your life using all of your resources to bring glory to God by serving others. On the other hand, after reading this book you might have the impression that good stewardship is about following rules, or remembering "to-do" lists. This could not be farther from the truth. Good stewardship is more about *being* than *doing*. Another way of saying this is that stewardship is a *process*, not an event.

We practice *event-focused stewardship* when our main concern is doing the right things. Certainly, there is much involved in stewardship which requires "doing," but if we only learn to do these things without focusing on our character, we miss the mark. Event-focused stewardship views what we do as a light switch—it's either on or off. With this wrong perspective, the only hope of hearing "well done" is living with the light of good stewardship turned on more often than it's off.

On the other hand, *process-focused stewardship* is concerned with being in a right relationship with God. When we are confident in God's love for us and His promises to work all things for our good and His glory, we are growing in our stewardship journey. The process-focused view understands that every Christian is a steward. It understands that we are all growing in our understanding and ability to steward God's resources well. With this view, stewardship is an important part of one's sanctification.

Next Steps

Well done! You're just about finished with this book, but your process of stewardship will be ongoing. The challenge now is for you to apply the principles we've taught throughout this book. You don't need to follow all of them, or implement everything all at once. Simply pick one or two ideas you feel will significantly impact your stewardship, and put them into practice. Reach out to our team if you would like to explore ways we could help you become an even better steward of your wealth.

Acknowledgements:

Roy and I would like to thank each person who was instrumental in the creation of the work. We especially want to thank our wives, Lana and Christine Russell, whose support and encouragement were exactly what we needed to get this book across the finish line.

We would also like to thank the entire team at The Life Financial Group for your dedication and support. Your hard work and commitment to the cause of Biblical Stewardship is helping to shape culture and in our own small way, make the world a better place. Thanks to Tyler Rutherford, Bekah Manwiller, and Drew Gysi for their help in organizing, editing, and driving this book project forward. Thanks also to Jeremy Ehst, Mark Magruder, Stephen Verkler, Angel Sotomayor, Stephen Rohrer, David Oxenford, Cheryl Gysi, Ashley Wegman, Annie Wegman, and Marshall Kissling for all your support.

Many thanks to our amazing clients and friends who have contributed to this work in innumerable ways through the years of faithful stewardship and dedication to the King of Kings and Lord of Lords. It is an honor to serve you and to call you friends.

About
Kharis Publishing:

Kharis Publishing, an imprint of Kharis Media LLC, is a leading Christian and inspirational book publisher based in Aurora, Chicago metropolitan area, Illinois. Kharis' dual mission is to give voice to under-represented writers (including women and first-time authors) and equip orphans in developing countries with literacy tools. That is why, for each book sold, the publisher channels some of the proceeds into providing books and computers for orphanages in developing countries so that these kids may learn to read, dream, and grow. For a limited time, Kharis Publishing is accepting unsolicited queries for nonfiction (Christian, self-help, memoirs, business, health and wellness) from qualified leaders, professionals, pastors, and ministers. Learn more at: https://kharispublishing.com/